uperstars *of* Autumn

Printed on Paper
Manufactured at
Westvaco's Luke Mill

Superstars of Autumn

**SEVENTY-FIVE
YEARS OF
THE NFL'S
GREATEST
PLAYERS**

Turner Publishing, Inc.

Published by Turner Publishing, Inc.
A Subsidiary of Turner Broadcasting System, Inc.
1050 Techwood Drive, N.W.
Atlanta, GA 30318

ISBN: 1-57036-104-5

Distributed by Andrews and McMeel
A Universal Press Syndicate Company
4900 Main Street
Kansas City, Missouri 64112

First Edition 10 9 8 7 6 5 4 3 2 1
Printed in the U.S.A.

IN PRAISE OF
FLESH AND BLOOD

Happy Anniversary, National Football League.

Seventy-five years old? My, how you've grown. It seems like just yesterday you were a scruffy kid with holes in your pants and not a whole lot of friends.

Yes, indeed, a lot has changed in the National Football League since 1920, from the equipment to the formations to the rules to the stadiums to the league's popularity. The players have changed, too.

Or have they?

They certainly are a lot bigger (or smaller, if you're talking about receivers) and faster, and all of those things that have resulted from intense scouting, year-round training, and proper diet. And, yes, they are paid a bit better than they used to be.

But some things never change, as they say, and one of those things is the competitive heart of an athlete. It still beats with the same rhythm, the same force with which it pounded when the ancient Greeks and Mayans were racing barefoot.

George Halas, who played in 1920, never got to watch Emmitt Smith, who was drafted by the Cowboys in 1990. The two men wouldn't seem to have much in common other than their NFL paychecks, but you can bet that when Halas walked onto a football field in his playing days, there was a feeling in his gut that was not unlike the sensation Smith has when he hears the roaring crowd at Texas Stadium.

It is an excitement, no doubt, perhaps even a little nervousness. But it is more. Every great NFL player has a confidence—sometimes quiet, sometimes otherwise—that tells him, "You will win your battles today because you are the best and because you deserve it."

Every one of the 75 players in this book heard that little voice. Some of them hear it still.

Seventy-five players for 75 seasons. They don't exactly compartmentalize into one player per year—and how could you select just one season for someone like Joe Montana, anyway?—but the symmetry seems appropriate.

Without these players, the NFL never could have grown into the most popular sports league in America, a measure that is backed up by television ratings, merchandise sales, and opinion polls.

You often hear it said that pro football boomed when television pervaded the American household, and there is no denying that the medium and the sport have been wedded with uncanny success. The NFL also has benefited from far-sighted leadership, and from the pure visual drama of the game.

But make no mistake about it. The NFL has achieved its dizzying position because of its players. Just as *Raging Bull* wouldn't have had the same impact had it starred your cousin

S U P E R S T A R S   O F   A U T U M N   5

Lenny, the NFL would have taken a different—and, almost certainly, sloppier—path without the likes of Ernie Nevers, Johnny Unitas, and Lawrence Taylor.

It is the great players who have kept fans watching with acrobatic catches, game-saving tackles, and breathtaking runs. More important, the great players have given pro football personality. Once you get past that athletic fire mentioned earlier, none of their stories are the same.

Red Grange, a one-man novelty, drew record-setting crowds in his first few NFL games; Night Train Lane, on the other hand, walked in off the street with a handful of newspaper clippings to ask the Los Angeles Rams for a job.

Don Hutson set the league on its ear on the first play of his second game, when he caught an 83-yard touchdown pass; Roger Staubach spent two full seasons biding time on the Dallas Cowboys' bench. Alan Page went to Notre Dame, the most storied football breeding ground in the nation; Dutch Clark sang the alma mater of Colorado College, and Deacon Jones came from Mississippi Vocational College.

Gale Sayers played only five healthy seasons, all of them unbelievable, before his knees betrayed him; George Blanda kicked footballs and threw occasional passes for 26 seasons, until he was 48 years old. Anthony Muñoz was a friendly giant of a man who didn't make enemies even of the defensive linemen he battered; Norm Van Brocklin was a tempestuous cuss who always seemed to be one minute away from an explosion.

They are tall, short (okay, medium-sized), stocky, and lean. They came from a hodgepodge of geographical areas, ethnic heritages, and circumstances.

Sammy Baugh rode horses and roped cattle on his family's ranch in Texas from the time he was old enough to walk. Chuck Bednarik flew 30 missions as a gunner on a B-24 Liberator bomber during World War II. Raymond Berry had one leg that was shorter than the other and his eyesight wasn't too good, none of which stopped him from becoming one of the finest receivers ever to play.

And then there was Johnny Blood. Demonstrating the breadth of backgrounds under the NFL shield, Blood spent varying amounts of time as an Air Corps sergeant, a cryptographer, a bartender, a prisoner in a Havana jail, a hotel desk clerk, a seaman, an accomplished debater, and a lauded poet. Oh, yes . . . and as a halfback and occasional coach.

People such as Johnny Blood are why this book was written. Because football isn't played in the strategy room or on TV or in rotisserie leagues. It's played on a 100-yard field. And if you peel away the helmets and pads and tape, you'll find it's still played by human beings with human qualities and human emotions.

Even if some of their athletic exploits seem superhuman.

—Phil Barber

Superstars of Autumn

Herb Adderley . . .

• Was all-NFL in 1962, 1963, 1965, 1966, and 1969, and played in five consecutive Pro Bowls (1964-68).

• Played on six NFL championship teams—three at Green Bay before the creation of the Super Bowl; two more with the Packers in Super Bowls I and II; and with the Cowboys, winners of Super Bowl VI. He also played with Dallas in Super Bowl V.

• Made the first interception return for a touchdown in a Super Bowl, going 60 yards against the Oakland Raiders in Super Bowl II.

• Averaged 22 yards per return on his 48 career interceptions, returning 7 for touchdowns. He also averaged 25.7 yards and had a pair of touchdowns on 120 kickoff returns.

• Returned 3 interceptions for touchdowns in 1965, tops in the NFL that season.

• Was enshrined in the Pro Football Hall of Fame in 1980.

Herb Adderley

CORNERBACK

Herb Adderley, with his great speed, marvelous reflexes, and a no-way-you-can-beat-me attitude, had few peers during his 12 seasons of playing left cornerback in the National Football League.

But he almost didn't get a chance to prove it. Adderley came to the Green Bay Packers as a number-one draft pick in 1961, following an excellent career as a running back at Michigan State. Unable to beat out Paul Hornung or Jim Taylor for a starting job, he toiled in the anonymity of special teams.

Then starting cornerback Hank Gremminger was injured during a Thanksgiving Day game at Detroit, and coach Vince Lombardi replaced him with Adderley, though the backup's only defensive experiences to that point were a brief stint as a middle safety in college and as a cornerback in the 1961 College All-Star Game. Adderley got his first career interception against the Lions that day and had the job for keeps when the 1962 season began.

"I was too stubborn to switch him to defense until I had to," Lombardi said. "Years later, it scared me to recall how I almost mishandled him."

Like most cornerbacks then, Adderley, at 6 feet 1 inch, 200 pounds, primarily played man-for-man coverage. Even late in his career with the Dallas Cowboys, during the 1971 season, he gave up only 3 touchdowns but had 6 interceptions. "I enjoyed going head-to-head with great receivers like Johnny Morris, Jimmy Orr, and Gary Collins," Adderley once said. "And I always wanted people who watched me play to say when they had left the stadium, 'He's the best cornerback I've ever seen.' "

Troy Aikman . . .

• **Was recruited at Oklahoma by current Cowboys coach Barry Switzer to help transform the Sooners from a Wishbone to pass-oriented team. But he transferred to UCLA when an injury put him on the sidelines and Switzer returned to the stacked backfield. Aikman finished his college career as the third-ranked passer in NCAA history.**

• **Joined Terry Bradshaw and Jim Plunkett as the only quarterbacks ever to be named Super Bowl MVP after being the first player selected in the NFL draft. Aikman got his award after Super Bowl XXVII.**

• **In 1993 had two three-game streaks in which he completed more than 70 percent of his passes, and he did it in another game as well.**

• **Reached 10,000 passing yards in 52 games, faster than any other quarterback in Cowboys history.**

• **Missed the first five games of his rookie season with a broken finger, but his fifth NFL game was spectacular: an NFL-rookie-record 379 yards against Phoenix.**

• **Had a 69.1-percent completion mark in 1993, a Dallas record.**

Every Dallas Cowboys quarterback since 1979 has fought equally hard to overcome NFL defenses and the ghost of Roger Staubach. So far, Troy Aikman is winning both battles.

Aikman has become "Young Man Winter" in Dallas because, like Hall-of-Fame member Staubach, he puts together his best string of performances during December and January, when NFL championships are decided. During those months in 1993 and 1994, as the Cowboys were heading toward back-to-back NFL titles, Aikman completed more than 71 percent of his passes for almost 3,000 yards, 26 touchdowns, and a 111.3 passer rating. Most important, he won eight of nine regular-season games to get his team into the playoffs.

He also became only the fifth quarterback ever to win consecutive Super Bowls, a far cry from the dog days of his rookie year, 1989, when he struggled with injuries and the Cowboys won just one game under new coach Jimmy Johnson.

Aikman is a splendidly accurate quarterback. He established a club record for lowest interception rate in a season (1.5 percent) in 1993 and once threw 151 consecutive passes without an interception, second best in club history. He also had a streak of 35 games in which he completed more than 50 percent of his passes.

Aikman's Super Bowl performances have been phenomenal. When the Cowboys buried the Buffalo Bills 52-17 in Super Bowl XXVII, he completed 22 of 30 passes for 273 yards and 4 touchdowns; and in Dallas's 30-13 victory over the Bills in Super Bowl XXVIII, he was 19 of 27 for 207 yards.

Lance Alworth . . .

• **Also was the number-one draft pick of the NFL's San Francisco 49ers for the 1962 season, but Al Davis, then an assistant coach at San Diego, got him to sign a contract before he played in the 1962 Sugar Bowl.**

• **Was the starting flanker for the Cowboys in Super Bowl VI. He caught a 7-yard touchdown pass in their victory over the Miami Dolphins.**

• **Won three pass-receiving titles in the old AFL.**

• **Was a fine high school baseball player who was offered contracts by both the New York Yankees and Pittsburgh Pirates.**

• **Caught just 35 passes in 1969, though he still was valuable enough to command three one-time starters—tight end Pettis Norman, tackle Tony Liscio, and defensive tackle Ron East—in a trade with Dallas in 1970.**

Lance Alworth

Lance Alworth was one of the great contradictions in NFL history. The wide receiver who was called "Bambi" was better suited for "Rocky."

The 6-foot, 184-pound former Arkansas All-America running back may have run like a deer (he covered 100 yards in 9.6 seconds), but that's where any resemblance to the lovable cartoon character ended. Alworth was as tough and resilient as any receiver in NFL history. He was absolutely fearless when roaming opposing secondaries in the San Diego Chargers' pass-happy offense, and he once played seven games—during which he caught 37 passes for 694 yards—with both hands hindered by fractures.

The Chargers made him the American Football League's first draft pick in 1962. A year later, he became the new league's first superstar on the strength of his surehandedness, speed, and ability to outleap opponents.

Alworth made the all-AFL team during each of that league's seven remaining seasons, played in seven AFL All-Star Games, and caught at least one pass in each of the 96 AFL games he played. When he retired after finishing his career with the Dallas Cowboys in 1971, he had amassed 542 catches for 10,266 yards, an 18.9-yard per-catch average, one of the best in NFL history. In 1978, he was inducted into the Pro Football Hall of Fame.

"A player comes along once in a lifetime who alone is worth the price of admission," record-setting receiver Charley Hennigan of the Houston Oilers once said. "Lance Alworth was that player."

Sammy Baugh . . .

• **Spent a summer as a minor-league shortstop in the St. Louis Cardinals' system, where his foremost rival was future major-league standout Marty Marion.**

• **Started Redskins Fever in his rookie season (1937), helping Washington begin a string of 40 consecutive sellouts at Griffith Stadium.**

• **Recorded his best season in 1947, when he completed 210 passes in 12 games, for 2,938 yards and 25 touchdowns.**

• **Was inducted into the Pro Football Hall of Fame in 1963 as a charter member.**

• **Cautioned an overzealous defensive lineman when the player roughed him up a couple of times. When the defender persisted, Baugh told his linemen to let the man through and hit him squarely in the face with a pass, knocking him out.**

• **Went "Hollywood" in the 1940s and played the lead in a serial called *King of the Texas Rangers*.**

• **Was the first head coach of the New York Titans (later called the Jets) of the American Football League.**

S ammy Baugh acquired the nickname "Slingin' Sam" the old-fashioned way—he earned it.

After two years as the ringmaster of Texas Christian University's famed "Aerial Circus" offense, Baugh joined the Washington Redskins as a number-one draft pick in 1937. For the next decade there was no better passer in the NFL.

A whip-lean Texan who could ride a horse and rope cattle but hated "city slicker" cowboy boots because they pinched his feet, Baugh immediately made his mark by winning the 1937 NFL passing title, one of six he won or shared. He led his team to a pair of NFL championships with victories over the Chicago Bears in 1937 and 1942, and also helped the Redskins win three other Eastern Division titles during 16 seasons in the NFL.

Baugh was one of the last great triple-threat backs. His passing made him famous, but he was a single-wing tailback until he became a T-formation quarterback; he played safety on defense, and his 11 interceptions led the NFL in 1943; he also won four consecutive punting titles from 1940–43 and is still the league's all-time leading punter with a career average of 45.1 yards. In the Redskins' 14-6 victory over Chicago in the 1942 NFL title game, his 85-yard quick-kick bottled up the Bears and set up Washington's first score.

Baugh's hallmarks were an ability to spread the ball accurately among different receivers (he had an NFL-record 70.3 completion percentage in 1945) and a determination to perform the unexpected. On a fourth-down play against Chicago in the 1937 championship game he stood in his end zone as if to punt but pulled off a beautiful fake with a 42-yard pass to Cliff Battles.

Chuck Bednarik . . .

• Benefited from a stroke of luck in becoming the Eagles' top pick in 1949. Philadelphia won the NFL title in '48 and was supposed to draft last. But the Eagles won the NFL's "bonus pick," an automatic first-round lottery choice, and used it to draft Bednarik.

• Was most valuable player of the 1954 Pro Bowl after recovering 3 fumbles, intercepting a pass, and punting for the East team when Charley Trippi was injured.

• Had 20 career interceptions for the Eagles, including 6 in 1953.

• Played against many of the NFL's greatest running backs, but he considered Browns fullback Marion Motley his toughest personal opponent: "He was 245 pounds, and when he gained momentum, he simply carried you with him."

• Was inducted into the Pro Football Hall of Fame in 1967, his first year of eligibility.

Chuck Bednarik is best remembered for one feat: In 1960 he became the last NFL player to play offense and defense for an entire game . . . actually, for four of them.

Five games into the season, Bednarik, who was already the Eagles' starting center, replaced injured Bob Pellegrini at left outside linebacker in a game at Cleveland. Bednarik then got double duty as a middle linebacker in back-to-back victories against the New York Giants and in the Eagles' 17-13 win over Green Bay in the 1960 NFL Championship Game.

He played 58 minutes against the Packers. In the game's final play, he collared Jim Taylor on a touchdown-saving tackle and sat on the fullback at Philadelphia's 8-yard line as the final seconds ticked off the clock.

Bednarik, a gunner in a B-24 Liberator bomber for 32 missions during World War II, joined the Eagles in 1949 after two seasons as an All-America at the University of Pennsylvania. He missed the first two games of his rookie season because coach Earle (Greasy) Neale didn't believe he was ready to play, but missed just one more for the rest of his 14-season career.

The Eagles' second-string center when they won the NFL title in 1949, Bednarik then was switched to linebacker, where he won all-NFL honors the next seven years.

He returned to center in 1957 and that's where he started the 1960 season until he was called upon for two-way duty. He played middle linebacker his last two seasons. Renowned for his aggressive play and aptly nicknamed "Concrete Charley" (he sold concrete during the offseason), Bednarik played in eight Pro Bowls.

Raymond Berry . . .

• Practiced the art of recovering a fumble every day in practice "just in case." No problem: He fumbled just once in his 13 seasons.

• Made 631 catches for 9,275 yards, a 14.7-yard average, and 68 touchdowns.

• Made three of his five Pro Bowl appearances from 1958–1960, leading the NFL in catches each year. His best overall season was 1960, when he made 74 catches for 1,298 yards. He had 75 receptions in 1961.

• Once estimated that he had 88 maneuvers to free himself of defensive coverage. And he practiced each move every week.

• Was head coach of the New England Patriots when they played in Super Bowl XX.

• Was inducted into the Pro Football Hall of Fame in 1973.

Raymond Berry wasn't a fast wide receiver by current standards. One of his legs was shorter than the other. His eyes weren't too good. All he did was work . . . and finish a 13-year NFL career with 631 receptions, an all-time record when he retired in 1967.

Berry had unusual leaping ability, hands like sponges, and a dogged sense of purpose. Turning pass receiving into a science, he worked with quarterback Johnny Unitas day after day in practice, running every route in the Baltimore Colts' playbook as if it had been drawn on the practice field. They became the NFL's most lethal combination, teaming for 600 completions.

After practice, when Unitas was exhausted, Berry cajoled anyone he could find—other teammates, coaches, equipment men, reporters, even his wife, Sally—into throwing him the ball.

Berry never was better than in the Colts' historic 23-17 overtime victory over the New York Giants in the 1958 NFL Championship Game, when he caught a postseason-record 12 passes for 174 yards and a touchdown. Three of the catches came on the drive that tied the score for the Colts in the final seven seconds and he caught 2 more for 33 yards on the winning overtime drive.

Berry was selected in the twentieth round of the 1954 NFL draft as a future pick, but many wondered why, since he had caught few passes at Southern Methodist in three years of competition and hadn't played regularly in high school until his senior year—despite his father being the head coach. Yet, by his third pro season he led the NFL with 800 receiving yards. He won the receiving title the next three seasons, twice finishing number one in yardage.

END

George Blanda . . .

• Played for two of the greatest football coaches in history. He was a linebacker, quarterback, punter, and placekicker for Paul (Bear) Bryant at Kentucky, and played for George Halas and the Bears for 10 years.

• Became the oldest quarterback ever to play in an NFL playoff game when, at age 43, he replaced the injured Daryle Lamonica and accounted for all of Oakland's points in a 27-17 loss to Baltimore in 1970.

• Had three consecutive 100-point seasons as a kicker for the Raiders (1967–69).

• Brought the Houston Oilers back from a 17-0 deficit to tie the score in the historic 1962 AFL Championship Game. Houston lost to the Dallas Texans 20-17 in double overtime.

• On his biggest regret: "I wish I could have played 'til I was fifty years old. That would have really been something. Gordie Howe did it in hockey."

• Played in 11 NFL/AFL/AFC title games and in Super Bowl II.

The numbers don't tell the entire story of George Blanda's pro football career: 2,002 points . . . 26,920 passing yards . . . 236 touchdown passes. But they certainly go a long way in characterizing a man who played through four decades, until he was a month shy of his forty-ninth birthday.

What epitomized Blanda's play most of all was a five-week stretch while playing for the Oakland Raiders in 1970. In successive games, he came off the bench and threw 3 touchdown passes in a win over Pittsburgh, kicked a 48-yard field goal to secure a tie against Kansas City, tossed a touchdown pass and kicked a 52-yard field goal in the final 94 seconds for a victory over Cleveland, threw a 20-yard scoring pass with 2:28 to play to beat Denver, and kicked the winning field goal with seven seconds left to defeat San Diego.

"People remember me for four or five games in Oakland," he once said, "but I can name you fifty before that that I won with a kick or a pass at the end. I hope people don't think 1970 was all I ever did."

Not by a long shot. After 10 seasons with the Chicago Bears, Blanda found new life in the newborn American Football League in 1960, leading the Houston Oilers to the AFL's first two titles. His 1961 championship drive was highlighted by two record-tying performances: 7 touchdown passes against the New York Titans and 36 touchdown passes for the season.

At age 40, he joined the Raiders, with whom he became America's best-known "senior citizen." In 1970, at age 43, Blanda won more postseason honors than any other NFL player.

How did he do it for so long?

"Think win," he said.

Johnny Blood . . .

• **Scored 37 touchdowns and 224 points in 15 seasons with five NFL teams.**

• **Got the inspiration for the name "Blood" when he and a friend passed a movie theater where the Rudolph Valentino classic** *Blood and Sand* **was playing. "I'll be 'Blood' and you be 'Sand,'" McNally told his friend, who also was trying to mask his true identity to play for pay on Sundays.**

• **Was known as the "Vagabond Halfback." At one time or another he was an Air Corps sergeant and cryptographer in China, a bartender, an overnight prisoner in a Havana jail, a hotel desk clerk, a seaman, an excellent debater, and an accomplished poet.**

• **Was known for outrageous antics. He once was late for a train scheduled to carry the Packers to an out-of-town game. Blood solved his dilemma by parking his car on the tracks as the train was about to leave, giving him enough time to get aboard.**

• **Was inducted into the Pro Football Hall of Fame as a charter member in 1963.**

The early NFL was often more fun off the field than it was on. Johnny Blood saw to that.

He was born John McNally, but when he played semipro games on Sundays while still a collegiate player at St. John's College in Minnesota, he devised the pseudonym "Johnny Blood" to protect his final year of eligibility. He kept the name throughout his 15-season career with five NFL teams.

Blood joined the NFL with the Milwaukee Badgers in 1925 but was still a star waiting to shine when he joined the Green Bay Packers in 1929. He was a fast, slashing inside runner who caught passes better than anyone in the fledgling league, and he was also a great defensive back and punter.

Blood played seven years in two stints at Green Bay, helping the Packers to four titles; he also dallied at Pottsville (Pennsylvania) and Pittsburgh, where he exasperated owner Art Rooney as both player and player-coach.

Actually, Blood exasperated practically everyone for whom he worked. His lusty enjoyment of the pleasures of life often obscured his achievements. Packers coach and general manager Curly Lambeau once offered him a contract for $110 per week if he promised not to drink after Tuesdays—or $100 without the incentive. Blood negotiated a Wednesday deadline for $110.

"Maybe the zodiac had it right," Blood once said. "I was born under Sagittarius. As I understand it, this made me part philosopher, part stud by decree of the stars. It is a helluva burden for a man to carry and practically impossible to live up to, although I don't deny making the attempt for a couple of years."

Terry Bradshaw . . .

• Was picked by the Steelers after they won a coin toss with the Chicago Bears to get the first pick in the 1970 draft.

• Was inducted into the Pro Football Hall of Fame in 1989.

• On his rough NFL start: "My rookie year was a disaster. I had no schooling on reading defenses. I had never studied the game films the way a quarterback should. I was an outsider who didn't mingle well. The other players looked at me as a bible-toting L'il Abner."

• Never saw the outcome of one of his most famous plays—a 64-yard touchdown pass to Lynn Swann in Super Bowl X. Hit by Dallas safety Cliff Harris, Bradshaw never saw Swann make a spectacular catch.

• Was known as a "streak" quarterback who could produce touchdowns and yards in big amounts. For instance, he had a touchdown pass in 12 of his team's first 13 games in 1976.

• Brought the Steelers from behind in three of their four Super Bowl victories.

T erry Bradshaw was the first quarterback to win four Super Bowls. Not bad for an athlete unfairly put down for being "too dumb."

The Pittsburgh Steelers chose Bradshaw with the first pick of the 1970 draft, and he became the most important building block used by coach Chuck Noll in constructing the NFL's best team of the '70s. Two years later, Bradshaw helped Pittsburgh win the first of eight AFC Central titles under Noll's direction, then earned lasting celebrity for completing the Immaculate Reception touchdown pass to Franco Harris that stunned the Oakland Raiders in the 1972 playoffs. Two years after that, Bradshaw led Pittsburgh to the first of four Super Bowl titles.

He seemed to be a throwback to another era because he was so physically tough. At 6 feet 3 inches and 210 pounds he was bigger than many running backs, and was just as punishing when he ran. He threw the ball 70 yards with a flick of his powerful wrist, but he also developed a laser-beam accuracy to wide receivers such as Lynn Swann and John Stallworth, producing 2,025 completions for 27,989 yards and 212 touchdowns over his 14-year NFL career.

Bradshaw always was at his best in the playoffs, amassing 30 touchdown passes and 3,833 yards in 19 postseason games. He was the most valuable player in Pittsburgh's victories in Super Bowls XIII and XIV. He was at his best in XIII with a 318-yard, 4-touchdown performance in the thrilling 35–31 victory over Dallas.

Jim Brown . . .

• **Was twice named the NFL's most valuable player, in 1958 and 1965.**

• **Was a unanimous all-NFL pick in eight of his nine seasons. He missed in 1962 when Jim Taylor of the NFL-champion Packers was chosen as the team's fullback.**

• **Played in the Pro Bowl after each of his nine seasons.**

• **Powered Cleveland to the 1964 NFL title. In an upset of the Baltimore Colts, he was the game's leading rusher with 114 yards on 27 carries.**

• **Set an NFL career record with 126 touchdowns.**

• **Had two magnificent 237-yard performances, during his rookie season of 1957 against the Rams and again in 1961 against Philadelphia.**

• **Lettered in football, basketball, track, and lacrosse at Syracuse.**

• **Stunned the NFL when he announced his retirement during the summer of 1966 to pursue a motion-picture career after filming *The Dirty Dozen* in England.**

Jim Brown is the greatest running back in NFL history—both to the majority of those who saw him play and to most who now must rely on NFL Films to re-create his prowess.

At 6 feet 2 inches and 228 pounds, Brown was the Cleveland Browns' fullback from 1957 through 1965, but he was really two backs rolled into one: He had sprinter's speed, with moves usually associated with swift, small halfbacks; and was even more renowned for his power, which allowed him to run over and through hordes of tacklers.

Brown's 12,312 rushing yards—in just nine seasons—was the elusive target of NFL running backs for 20 years until Walter Payton broke the career mark in 1984. Brown has been also surpassed by Tony Dorsett and Eric Dickerson, but all three needed more games and seasons, and none of them are close to another measurement of running ability—Brown's record 5.2 yards per carry.

Paul Brown, head coach of the Browns for six of the fullback's seasons, called him "a once-in-a-lifetime player who became the best running back ever to play professional football." And the coach had seen all three players who broke Jim Brown's career rushing record.

Brown led NFL rushers a record eight times and topped 1,000 yards in seven of his nine seasons, missing the mark by just 4 yards in 1962, and by 58 yards in his 12-game rookie year. His best season was a then-record 1,863 yards in 1963. He was inducted into the Hall of Fame in 1971.

An admiring opponent put it best: "That Brown. He says he isn't Superman. What he really means is that Superman isn't Jimmy Brown."

Dick Butkus . . .

• **Was an unselfish contributor who returned 12 kickoffs and once rushed 28 yards on a fake punt. He even scored the deciding point in a game against Washington when he leaped high in the end zone to catch a desperation pass after a botched conversion attempt.**

• **Played in eight Pro Bowls and was elected to the Pro Football Hall of Fame in 1979, his first year of eligibility.**

• **Was once voted by a panel of NFL coaches as the one player they would want above all others to start a new franchise.**

• **Had his own way of psyching himself for a game: "When I went out on the field to warm up, I would manufacture things to make me mad. If someone on the other team was laughing, I'd pretend he was laughing at me or the Bears."**

• **Had his top interception season as a rookie in 1965, when he had 5.**

During the last half of the 1960s and the early 1970s, no NFL linebacker put more of himself into his job than Dick Butkus. The 6-foot 3-inch, 245-pound middle linebacker of the Chicago Bears retired after the 1973 season, but he has gained a couple of new generations of fans who have seen the highlights of his work in NFL Films productions shown on cable television.

From the very start of his career, he made clear his ambition: "When they say all-pro middle linebacker, I want them to mean Butkus."

He did it by playing in the highest tradition of "The Monsters of the Midway." When he ran sideline to sideline, crashed through a wall of blockers, or filled a hole to tackle a running back, Butkus snarled and growled. He talked trash and he backed it up with bone-jarring tackles.

Butkus was a number-one draft choice of both the Bears and the AFL's Denver Broncos in 1965. He chose the Bears so he could play in his hometown, and he made Chicago fans happy in his first game with 11 unassisted tackles against the San Francisco 49ers.

When Butkus finished after just nine seasons, betrayed by an injured right knee, he had accumulated 47 defensive takeaways (25 fumble recoveries, 22 interceptions) and had made the all-NFL team seven times. "Football is something I was made for," Butkus said. "I guess my only regret is that my career was too short."

It wasn't for those who faced him. "If I had a choice, I'd sooner go one-on-one with a grizzly bear," Packers running back MacArthur Lane once said. "I pray that I can get up every time Butkus hits me."

Earl Campbell . . .

• **Was once described this way by Hall-of-Fame defensive tackle Joe Greene of Pittsburgh: "He could inflict more damage on a team than any back I ever faced. He was a punishing runner who physically hurt you."**

• **Finished his NFL career with the New Orleans Saints and his first Oilers coach, Bum Phillips.**

• **Never made it to the Super Bowl, but he came close, playing in two losses to the Pittsburgh Steelers in consecutive AFC title games (1978–79).**

• **Was the eleventh Heisman Trophy winner to become the first player picked in the NFL draft.**

• **Played in five Pro Bowls and was all-pro and all-AFC in 1978, '79, and '80.**

• **Gained 1,934 yards in 1980, the third-highest figure in NFL history.**

• **Became the first rookie to lead the NFL in rushing (1,450 yards in 1978) since Jim Brown did it 21 seasons earlier.**

Earl Campbell was a force unto himself when he came to the Houston Oilers in 1978 as the NFL's number-one pick, and he more than lived up to his top billing as he became:

• NFL most valuable player,
• NFL rookie of the year,
• NFL rushing leader, and
• member of the NFL all-pro team.

Most had projected Campell as a full-time fullback when he left the University of Texas, but before his rookie season had ended, he had played fullback, halfback, and tailback in the I-Formation. His 36-inch thighs, 4.6 speed, and 5-foot 11-inch, 244-pound frame were tailor-made for all of those positions.

The "Tyler Rose" led all NFL rushers in each of his first three seasons and was first in the AFC in his fourth. He gained 1,000 yards in five of his first six years, posting eleven 100-yard games in 1979 and four 200-yard games in 1980.

He reached almost legendary status even before the end of his rookie season with a memorable 199-yard, 4-touchdown performance in a nationally televised Monday-night game against the Miami Dolphins. He capped the game with an 81-yard touchdown run on a sweep that he punctuated with a beautiful move that left the last defender grasping at air.

Campbell took on every tackler. The front of his thighs took a fearsome beating, probably costing him two or three more seasons of peak production. Still, in nine seasons he won three NFL most-valuable-player awards, gained 9,407 rushing yards, and earned a place in the Pro Football Hall of Fame.

Dutch Clark . . .

• Completed 53.6 percent of his passes for the Lions in 1936, when the league average was 36.5 percent.

• Led the NFL in scoring three times.

• Along with teammates Ace Gutowski, Ernie Caddel, and Glenn Presnell, was part of the NFL's best running game from 1934–36. After winning the NFL title in 1935, the Lions rolled up 2,885 rushing yards in '36, a record that lasted 36 years.

• Was head coach of the Lions in 1937 and 1938, then spent four years as assistant coach with the Cleveland Rams.

• Gained 2,757 rushing yards, 4.8 per carry, during six of his seven NFL seasons in which the league kept official statistics.

Dutch Clark

If Earl (Dutch) Clark wasn't a charter enshrinee in the Pro Football Hall of Fame, you almost could say he had a silent career.

He had played for tiny Colorado College, and Alan Gould, sports editor of the *Associated Press*, bypassed far more visible players from larger schools to name him to the 1929 All-America team. Clark was almost embarrassed by the sudden burst of unwanted fame. It took him two years to dredge up enough nerve to join the NFL's Portsmouth Spartans in 1931 to see if he could play at a higher level.

He could. Clark was the 1931 NFL rookie of the year for Portsmouth. Stationed along the Ohio River, the Spartans had only 14 players and drew three times as many people to watch a free practice than paying customers to watch a game.

After two seasons, Clark disappeared for one year to coach Colorado College. When he returned in 1934, the Spartans had moved to Detroit and become the Lions—and Clark proved he had gotten better during his sabbatical.

"Dutch is like a rabbit in a brush heap," his Lions coach, George (Potsy) Clark (no relation), once said. "When he gets into the secondary, he has no plan, just instinct. Just when you expect him to be smothered, he's free of his tacklers."

Dutch Clark was an all-NFL quarterback six times, judged at that position because he called his team's plays. He was so self-effacing that his teammates said he practically blushed every time he called one for himself, despite being a triple-threat star who ran, passed, and was considered the NFL's best all-around kicker, the last of the full-time drop-kick artists.

Eric Dickerson . . .

• **Was part of SMU's famed "Pony Express" backfield in the early 1980s, teaming with future NFL runner Craig James, now a commentator for ESPN.**

• **Was a number-one pick of both the Los Angeles Rams and the Arizona Wranglers of the USFL in 1983.**

• **Was the focal point of one of the biggest trades in NFL history when he went to the Indianapolis Colts midway through the 1987 season for one first- and two second-round draft picks, plus running back Owen Gill. When the three-team deal was complete, linebacker Cornelius Bennett was in Buffalo and the Rams had running back Greg Bell and a slew of draft choices.**

• **Spent five seasons with the Colts and helped them win the 1987 AFC Eastern Division title and make their first playoff appearance since moving from Baltimore.**

• **Went to Los Angeles when the Raiders traded fourth- and eighth-round draft choices to Indianapolis in 1992.**

• **Played in four Pro Bowls.**

Eric Dickerson is the second-ranked rusher in pro football history, and rarely has the sport seen a runner who combined such grace and power in his running style.

At 6 feet 3 inches and 220 pounds, Dickerson ran the 100-yard dash in 9.3 seconds, and he seemed to glide over the ground rather than tear it up. He seldom appeared to be moving fast, yet he gained 13,259 yards in 11 seasons.

Dickerson crashed into the NFL with the Los Angles Rams in 1983, setting rookie records with 390 attempts for 1,808 yards and 18 touchdowns. His first three games were modest, but within a five-week span he lit up the Jets for 192 yards, the Lions for 199, and the 49ers for 142- and 144-yard days.

But Dickerson's footsteps became a mighty roar in 1984 when he set a single-season rushing record with 2,105 yards, breaking the record of his good friend, O. J. Simpson, who had 2,003 in 1973. Dickerson had an NFL-record twelve 100-yard games that year. "He is the best I've seen, and I mean ever," Simpson said.

Rams coach John Robinson, who had enjoyed similar success with a tailback-oriented attack at the University of Southern California, let Dickerson loose. In slightly more than four seasons with the Rams, the former SMU star gained more than 7,000 rushing yards.

He had an NFL-record seven consecutive 1,000-yard seasons with the Rams and the Indianapolis Colts, never gaining less than 1,200 yards in any of those years. Unfortunately, contract disputes with both the Rams and Colts marred an otherwise brilliant career.

Mike Ditka . . .

• Became the first tight end ever inducted into the Pro Football Hall of Fame in 1988.

• Was an All-America at Pitt, where he played tight end and linebacker and was also one of the nation's top punters during his three varsity seasons.

• Was also the first draft pick of the AFL's Houston Oilers in 1961.

• Caught 427 passes for 5,812 yards and 43 touchdowns during his NFL career.

• Played in five consecutive Pro Bowls (1962–66) and was picked to the all-NFL team four times.

• Played for the Philadelphia Eagles in 1967–68, then joined the Cowboys for his final four seasons, playing in Super Bowls V and VI. He started at tight end in Super Bowl VI and caught a 7-yard touchdown pass from Roger Staubach.

• Was christened Michael Dyzcko before the family Anglicized the name to Ditka.

• Was the Bears' head coach when they won Super Bowl XX. He won a total of 112 games in 11 seasons, second only to George Halas in club history.

Mike Ditka was born to play tight end . . . or linebacker . . . or offensive tackle— any position that required contact and intensity.

Ditka was a pioneer as an NFL tight end, the first to become a consistent downfield receiving threat. In his rookie season with the Chicago Bears in 1961, he caught 56 passes for 1,076 yards and a 12 touchdowns. What made him doubly valuable were his great blocking skills, which had been the primary duty of most tight ends before him.

Ditka never surpassed his rookie numbers during his 12-year career with Chicago, Philadelphia, and Dallas, but for most of those seasons, he was the best all-around tight end in the NFL. He helped the Bears win the NFL title in 1963 and the Dallas Cowboys win the crown in Super Bowl VI.

In '63, he had a 4-touchdown day against the Rams and was credited with the key play in five of the Bears' victories. He then set up the clinching score in the championship game against the Giants.

Ditka loved contact. Bears coach George Halas said his tight end had one of the strongest stiff-arm moves after catching the ball he ever had seen; And Ditka was tough—en route to playing in 84 consecutive games, he ignored a leg injury that doctors said would have required surgery on most players.

Regarding his fierce competitiveness, Ditka once said: "I just try to hit the other guy before he hits me, and if I hit hard enough, maybe he won't want to hit me back."

Tony Dorsett . . .

• **Had a spectacular career at the University of Pittsburgh. He was an All-America as a freshman, junior, and senior; he finished as the all-time NCAA rushing leader with 6,082 yards; and he capped his career by winning the Heisman Trophy.**

• **Joined the Cowboys when they pulled off a draft-day deal to get him as the second overall pick in 1977, sending a first-round choice and three second-rounders to Seattle, which held the spot.**

• **Capped his first season by being selected rookie of the year and helping the Cowboys to their second NFL title with a victory over Denver in Super Bowl XII.**

• **Had his best season in 1981, when he gained a club-record 1,646 yards, with nine 100-yard games.**

• **Played in two Super Bowls, five NFC title games, and four Pro Bowls.**

• **Played his final season with Denver under his friend and former Dallas assistant coach Dan Reeves.**

• **Was elected to the Pro Football Hall of Fame in 1994, his first year of eligibility.**

Tony Dorsett was called "TD," and the nickname was apt. He is the third-leading rusher in NFL history; his 91 touchdowns are exceeded by only eight other running backs in NFL history; and he holds the record for the NFL's longest run from scrimmage, a 99-yard touchdown against the Minnesota Vikings—when his Dallas Cowboys had only 10 men on the field!

Because Dorsett was no giant at 5 feet 11 inches, 185 pounds, coach Tom Landry limited his per-game carries at the outset of his career. Dorsett bristled because he was competing with workhorses such as Earl Campbell, Walter Payton, and Wilbert Montgomery at the time. But Landry was adamant—and while it may have cost Dorsett some NFL rushing titles, it turned out to be a career-lengthening decision.

"If I wanted to risk Tony, I think he could gain as many yards as Payton and Campbell," Landry said at the time.

Dorsett played 12 seasons, 11 with the Cowboys and one with Denver, finishing with 12,739 yards. He was the first runner ever to gain 1,000 yards in his first five seasons, and he did it eight times in nine years. He gained 100 or more yards in 46 games, and the Cowboys won 42 of them.

"What impressed me about Dorsett was his tenacity," Landry said. "You could contain him for three quarters, but he would keep after it and break a long one to beat you in the fourth quarter."

Dorsett was a swift, smooth runner. Defenders rarely got a head-on shot at him because he hit the hole faster than any back in the league and used sharp, crisp cuts and cutbacks to get into the clear.

John Elway . . .

- Was the first pick of the Baltimore Colts (and the first overall) in 1983, but he refused to play for then-coach Frank Kush and forced a trade to Denver for quarterback Mark Herrmann, offensive tackle Chris Hinton, and a number-one selection.

- Has a football father. Jack Elway coached at San Jose State when John played at nearby Stanford, and later coached the Cardinal and the Frankfurt Galaxy of the World League.

- Was a two-time All-America selection at Stanford, where he graduated with a degree in economics.

- Notched his best yardage performance in 11 seasons when he passed for 432 yards against Seattle in 1985.

- Has been named to four Pro Bowls and has played in three.

- Twice was drafted by major league teams, the Kansas City Royals in 1979 and the New York Yankees in 1981. A second-round pick of the Yankees, he spent a summer with their Oneonta (New York) farm club in the Rookie League, where he played the outfield and batted .318.

John Elway

J ohn Elway may be the most exciting quarterback in the NFL today. Without a doubt, he is the man opposing coaches fear most with the game on the line in the fourth quarter.

Elway has brought the Denver Broncos from behind to victory 31 times in 11 seasons, more than any quarterback in NFL history. Who can forget his magnificent performance in what has become known as The Drive—a 98-yard, 15-play march in the final two minutes that forged a last-second tie against the Cleveland Browns in the 1986 playoffs? That possession was so dramatic that the nine-play, 60-yard drive for the winning field goal in overtime that gave Denver the AFC title seemed almost anti-climactic.

Elway repeated the act in a different form against Houston in the 1991 playoffs. He rallied his team from a 21-6 fourth-quarter deficit to a 26-24 victory, again marching his team 98 yards on the winning drive. He twice made fourth-down plays, to keep Denver alive, running 7 yards for one first down and passing 44 yards to Vance Johnson to set up the winning field goal.

But there is more to Elway than fourth-quarter heroics. In 1993 he had his first 4,000-yard passing season and his eighth of more than 3,000 yards. He has gained more than 36,000 yards of offense, including 2,435 by rushing, eighth best among all NFL quarterbacks.

The only cloud in his career has been Elway's inability to win in three Super Bowl appearances—though in each case his team has been physically overmatched against NFC opponents.

Frank Gifford . . .

• Was an All-America at USC, and was picked to play in both the North-South and East-West All-Star Games following his college career. He played 60 minutes in both games as an offensive and defensive back.

• Was a first-round pick of the New York Giants in 1952.

• Was named to the Pro Bowl team six consecutive years, the first time as a defensive back in 1953, the others as a running back.

• Was inducted into the Pro Football Hall of Fame in 1977.

• Was leveled by the crushing blindside tackle of Eagles linebacker Chuck Bednarik in 1960. Gifford missed the rest of that season and 1961 as well, but he returned to finish his career as a flanker from 1962–64.

• Also accounted for 14 touchdowns on 60 run-pass option plays during his career; he even handled some placekicking in 1953 and 1956.

• Later added to his national popularity with play-by-play and commentary on ABC's "Monday Night Football."

F rank Gifford was the kind of handsome football player movie script writers used to make into heroes. It wouldn't have taken much imagination to concoct a script for him, either—all they had to do was use his real career.

Gifford was one of the most versatile players in the NFL. He came to the New York Giants as a number-one draft choice in 1952 after starring at USC where he was a Single-Wing tailback and a T-formation quarterback who ran and passed with excellence; he also played defense, placekicked, and punted.

Gifford did most of the above with the Giants. In his second NFL season, he played defense and made the Pro Bowl. The following year, he went to that game as a running back, the first time that ever happened. In his first nine seasons with the Giants, he was the team's star running back. For the last three, he was their starting flanker.

The NFL came of age in large part because the Giants attracted wide attention in New York City after they won the 1956 championship, and Gifford became the league's poster boy. He had good speed, but was an intelligent runner who picked his way through defenses to gain more than 3,700 rushing yards and score 34 touchdowns in his role as the "go-to" runner. In 1956 he became the first NFL player ever to finish in the top 10 in both rushing and receiving when his 819 rushing yards ranked fifth and his 51 catches for 603 yards was third. He did it again the following year.

When Gifford moved to flanker in 1962, he added to a receiving career that totaled more than 5,000 yards and 40 touchdowns. In 1962, teaming with Pro Football Hall-of-Fame quarterback Y. A. Tittle for the first time, he averaged 20 yards on 36 catches.

Frank Gifford

HALFBACK-FLANKER

Otto Graham . . .

• Ushered in a new invention after having his face smashed in a game during the 1954 season. To allow him to play the next week, coach Paul Brown and the helmet manufacturer devised a protective bar, which evolved into the facemask now worn by all NFL players.

• Had been an All-America tailback at Northwestern, but in beating Brown's Ohio State team in 1941, he impressed the coach with his peripheral vision and ability to throw the football accurately from any point on the field. That's why Graham was the first player Brown signed to a pro contract, and why the coach paid him a retainer while he still was in the Navy during World War II.

• Avenged two consecutive NFL title-game losses to Detroit when he scored 3 touchdowns and passed for 3 more in Cleveland's smashing 56-10 win over the Lions for the 1954 championship.

• Also played professional basketball with Rochester of the National Basketball League during his early years in pro football.

P aul Brown was adamant when he talked about Otto Graham.

"Otto is the greatest player in the game's history," Brown said. "Playing the most important position—quarterback—he guided our teams into the playoff finals every year of his ten seasons in professional football, seven times helping us win championships. No other player has ever achieved this."

It's hard to argue with the point offered by Brown, the Cleveland Browns' coach during Graham's 10 seasons as quarterback of the team. Graham led the Browns to every championship in the four-year history of the All-America Football Conference. Disdained for their AAFC play, Graham and the Browns stunned the NFL when they won the title in 1950, their first year in the league. They then played in the NFL Championship Game the next five seasons, winning in 1954 and 1955.

Graham, 6 feet 1 inch and 195 pounds, was a master T-formation passer who ran the Browns' intricate passing game so well that he earned the nickname "Automatic Otto." For three decades after retiring, he was pro football's top-ranked passer.

Graham completed 58 percent of his passes for 23,584 yards and 174 touchdowns at a time when seasons were only 12 games. In all, he had a 105-17-4 regular-season record.

Half the time his directions to teammates simply were "check with me," meaning that Graham called the play when he got to the line of scrimmage—and his calls usually were correct.

The results were 10 seasons worth of championships . . . and a spot in the Pro Football Hall of Fame.

Red Grange . . .

- **Played in three NFL title games with the Bears, including the famed 1932 indoor championship at Chicago Stadium in which the Bears beat the Portsmouth Spartans 9-0; and the renowned "Sneakers Game," which the Bears lost to the Giants in 1934, spoiling their perfect season.**

- **Visited Washington on his 1925 tour with the Bears and was invited to the White House to meet President Calvin Coolidge. Grange's introduction to Coolidge as a member of the Chicago Bears elicited the now-famous reply, "Glad to meet you. I always did enjoy animal acts."**

- **Returned to the Bears in 1929, partly because he had been wiped out financially early in the Great Depression. He sold insurance door-to-door after the football season, and ultimately regained financial solvency.**

- **Was the Michael Jordan of his day. There hardly was a product that he didn't endorse when he began his pro career in 1925—Red Grange dolls, Red Grange sweaters, Red Grange candy bars, Red Grange shoes . . . even Red Grange meat loaf.**

Harold (Red) Grange, the "Galloping Ghost" during brilliant seasons at the University of Illinois, made his biggest contribution to professional football as the star of an exhausting coast-to-coast barnstorming tour with the Chicago Bears in 1925.

Over two months, some 400,000 spectators watched Grange and the Bears as part of a plan hatched by Bears co-owner and coach George Halas to inject a quick fix of income and notoriety for his team and his young league, the NFL. Grange and his manager, C. C. (Cash-and-Carry) Pyle, signed a contract to play for the Bears shortly after his career at Illinois had ended.

The tour started at Chicago's Wrigley Field on Thanksgiving Day as 36,000 watched the Bears play the crosstown Cardinals, and it later included crowds of 73,000 at New York's Polo Grounds and 75,000 at the Los Angeles Coliseum.

Pyle demanded that Grange be given his own NFL franchise in New York in 1926. The NFL refused, so Pyle and Grange established the American Football League and he played there anyway. That venture was short-lived. A serious knee injury then kept Grange out of football in 1928, and he rejoined the Bears in '29.

The injury robbed him of his great open-field moves for the last six seasons of his career. Grange became basically a straight-ahead runner and actually was better as a defensive player. In that role he helped Chicago win two NFL titles, including a victory over the Giants in the 1933 NFL Championship Game, a win Grange preserved with a last-second tackle.

HALFBACK

Joe Greene . . .

• **Was the first draft pick selected by Chuck Noll in 1969, Noll's rookie coaching season. It paid off as Greene was chosen NFL defensive rookie of the year and voted to the Pro Bowl, the first of 10 appearances.**

• **Was a brute from the start of his NFL career. Veteran offensive linemen Ray Mansfield and Bruce Van Dyke decided to teach him a "lesson" during his rookie training camp, with a high/low double-team block. "He grabbed Bruce by the neck and me by my shoulder pads and tossed both of us away like we were rag dolls, and then it took him about a half-second to get to the quarterback,"** Mansfield recalled.

• **Didn't really like his nickname, "Mean Joe." It was a takeoff on the nickname of his college team, the Mean Green of North Texas State, but Greene felt it misrepresented the way he played.**

• **Was either all-pro or all-AFC every year of the 1970s except 1978, and was NFL most valuable defensive player in 1972 and 1974.**

• **Was inducted into the Pro Football Hall of Fame in 1987.**

D riving for their first division title in 1972, the Pittsburgh Steelers were tied 3-3 with the Oilers when Steelers defensive tackle Joe Greene turned to linebacker Andy Russell and said, "The defense is going to win this game."

He didn't say he, personally, was going to win it, but he could have. Greene blocked a field goal, recovered a fumble that set up the Steelers' winning score, then turned aside a late Oilers threat by sacking quarterback Dan Pastorini on three consecutive plays. He had 5 sacks in the game.

"He was the best I've seen," Steelers coach Chuck Noll later said. "Joe set the standard for us. Physically, he had all the necessary attributes, but he also set the standard for attitude. There will never be another Joe Greene. Joe will always be something special."

Greene was the leader of Pittsburgh's famed "Steel Curtain" defense that helped the team win four Super Bowls in the 1970s. He was quick; he was strong and determined; and he was the boss.

He also was the first to take an angled stance between the center and guard, completely disrupting offensive blocking schemes because he got into the gap so quickly. That strategy played a large part in his accumulating 66 sacks, 10 fumble recoveries, and an interception during his 13-season career.

The "other" side of Greene was clearly evident in an award-winning Coca-Cola commercial that showed a weary Mean Joe interacting with a young fan. As the boy turned to walk away, Joe yelled, "Hey, kid," and he tossed him his jersey. That brief scene later became the genesis of a made-for-TV movie, *The Steeler and the Pittsburgh Kid.*

Forrest Gregg

Forrest Gregg . . .

• Played for six NFL champions, his last as a member of the 1971 Dallas Cowboys, his third Super Bowl winner.

• Was very durable, playing in 188 consecutive games between 1956 and 1971.

• Was head coach of the 1981 AFC-champion Cincinnati Bengals, making him the first Super Bowl player ever to return to the game as head coach. (The Bengals lost to San Francisco in Super Bowl XVI.) Gregg also was head coach of the Cleveland Browns and Green Bay Packers.

• Retired in 1963 to take job as line coach at Tennessee, but Packers coach Vince Lombardi coaxed him back. Gregg retired again in 1970 after two years as player-coach, but when the Cowboys needed offensive line help he signed with them—and took home his third Super Bowl ring.

• Said he tried to model his offensive tackle play after Hall-of-Fame member Bob St. Clair of the 49ers: "He was the best I ever saw."

• Was elected to the Hall of Fame in 1977.

Vince Lombardi once called tackle Forrest Gregg "the finest player I ever coached."

There could be no higher praise from one of the NFL's greatest coaches, but it also was an appreciation from one former offensive lineman (Lombardi was one of Fordham's famed "Seven Blocks of Granite") to the work ethic of another.

No one labored harder than Gregg, who came to the Packers in 1956 hoping to be a defensive lineman. Assistant coach Lyle Blackbourn made him an offensive tackle, although even by 1956 NFL standards, he was small at 6 feet 4 inches, 220 pounds.

But Gregg took the challenge. He built himself up to 250 pounds and studied the techniques of the great offensive linemen, looking for help; he also studied the techniques of the defenders he would face, looking for ways to beat them.

Gregg said later that he was helped by having to work against Pro Football Hall-of-Fame defensive end Willie Davis every day in practice during his seasons at Green Bay. "After Willie, nearly everyone else was easy," he said. "He kept me sharp and he taught me a lot about what to expect from other defensive ends."

Gregg was tenacious, tough, and unselfish, even swinging to guard for portions of 1961 and 1965 when the Packers were beset by injuries. It meant learning new techniques and playing against defensive tackles instead of defensive ends. But it never affected his play.

He was an all-NFL lineman eight consecutive years; in 1965 he was picked a guard by one wire service and a tackle by another. Gregg played in nine Pro Bowls.

George Halas . . .

• Was a three-sport star at the University of Illinois, where he began his football career as a running back but was shifted to end by coach Bob Zuppke.

• Entered the Navy in 1919 and was accorded second-team All-America status while playing end for the Great Lakes Naval Training Center. He made 2 touchdown receptions and intercepted a pass in the 1919 Rose Bowl as Great Lakes defeated Mare Island Navy 17-0.

• Was a budding major league outfielder who saw his career with the New York Yankees nipped in his first spring training camp in 1919. A leg injury kept him from playing regularly and eventually caused him to spend the rest of the season in the minor leagues. He was replaced, believe it or not, by Babe Ruth.

• Won 324 games, 6 NFL championships, and 10 Western Conference titles during four decades as head coach of the Bears. He had two teams with perfect regular-season records, and six others that lost just one game.

eorge (Papa Bear) Halas was the founder of the Chicago Bears and a pioneer of the National Football League. But what about George Halas the player, an end for the Bears, née Decatur/Chicago Staleys, from the time he formed the team in 1920 until 1929?

Halas was hired as athletic director of the A. E. Staley Company, of Decatur, Illinois, to sign employee-athletes and coach them on the company's baseball and football teams. Each player, himself included, was paid $75 per game, a princely sum for semipros at that time.

Halas the football player was much like Halas the coach and owner—scrappy, defiant, and at 6 feet, 170 pounds, not afraid to mix it up with anyone (though he fondly recalled fleeing one postgame melee in Rock Island, Illinois, in 1920, first on foot, and then by taxi to get across the state line into Iowa).

Halas was a tenacious blocker, which was the primary job of an end at that time. He was tough, once playing an entire game with a broken jaw. He was a nuisance on defense because he used every tactic of the day—and the rules, right and wrong, were vaguely enforced—in going after runners.

His crowning moment occurred in 1923 when he recovered a fumble by Jim Thorpe of the Oorang Indians and returned it 98 yards for a touchdown, a record that lasted half a century.

"I probably ran 198 yards," Halas once recalled, "because I zigged and zagged all the way down the field, almost sideline to sideline, to keep Thorpe away from me. He was so close at times I could almost feel his breath."

John Hannah . . .

• Has the NFL in his genes. His father, Herb, played for the New York Giants in 1951, and his brother Charley was a third-round pick of the Tampa Bay Buccaneers. Charley also played for the Raiders.

• Had two All-America seasons at Alabama.

• Weighed 285 pounds at Alabama, making him the biggest player in that school's storied football history when he left. In the spring, when he put the shot, he often weighed 300 pounds, but he played at 260-270 in the NFL to preserve his quickness.

• Was voted the NFL's best offensive lineman several times by his peers.

• Won the praise of Raiders coach and current TV analyst John Madden, who once said that Hannah would be the first player he chose if he were starting a pro team from scratch.

• Played in the 1977 Pro Bowl, then was selected eight years in a row from 1979–1986.

J ohn Hannah's philosophy was simple and he repeated it many times during his 13 seasons as an offensive lineman for the New England Patriots. "I went into a game thinking, 'I'm going to win this game with a great play, the big block at the right time,'" he said. "I thought to myself before every play that 'This could be it, and the play I make right now could win it for us.'"

Hannah often made good on that vow. He is considered the best guard of his generation, fully justifying the Patriots' decision to make him a number-one pick in 1973, though he had little pass-blocking experience.

"He was an easy choice coming out of college," Patriots vice president and former personnel director Bucko Kilroy said. "He had the perfect size for a great guard in the pros. He also had the quickness of some running backs and 4.8 speed in the forty-yard dash."

Hannah was a fearsome drive blocker who sparked the Patriots' running game, particularly in 1978 when it set an all-time NFL record of 3,165 yards. He was an awesome sight leading a play through a hole or around the corner, as he took aim at linebackers and defensive backs. Sometimes they would just dive out of his way.

Hannah's early pass-blocking shortcomings were largely a result of playing in Bear Bryant's Wishbone system at Alabama, where the forward pass was an afterthought. Hannah's great strength and tenacity helped him through some rough times. And because he was "short-armed," he adjusted his game again when the rules were changed to allow offensive blockers to extend their arms fully when fending off pass rushers.

Franco Harris . . .

• Was one of nine children of a black father and Italian mother. He was the only player in NFL history to have his own "army"—Franco's Italian Army, from a mixed Pittsburgh neighborhood of Italians and blacks.

• Voted to nine consecutive Pro Bowls (1973–1981).

• Had a great 1972 rookie season, all the more remarkable considering that he carried just 26 times in his first four games. After exploding for 115 yards in the fifth game, he ran off six 100-yard games in a row, the longest such streak of his career.

• Is one of six players with 100 touchdowns (he had an even century).

• Had 100 or more rushing yards in 47 games. His receiving skills upped his combined yardage to 14,622 yards, sixth all time.

• Finished the last season of his career with the Seattle Seahawks after leaving Pittsburgh in a salary dispute.

• Was elected to the Pro Football Hall of Fame in 1990.

Franco Harris

Franco Harris keyed the Pittsburgh Steelers' awesome running game during the 1970s when they won four Super Bowls.

At 6 feet 2 inches and 225 pounds, Harris was a strong, powerful runner with good speed and open-field cutback moves. He exploded on the scene by rushing for 1,055 yards in his 1972 rookie season. When he retired after the 1983 season, he ranked fourth all time among NFL rushers with 12,120 yards. He had eight 1,000-yard seasons, holding or sharing 24 NFL rushing records.

Always at his best in the playoffs, Harris ran for 1,556 yards and 16 touchdowns (he also had 1 scoring reception) in 19 playoff games. He was named most valuable player after gaining a record-setting 154 rushing yards against Minnesota in Super Bowl IX.

Harris was conscious of avoiding injury, both in practice and in games. Despite his great power, he preferred to run out of bounds rather than trying to flatten a tackler when he believed it would be to no avail. He missed only nine games with injuries during his career.

No one knew precisely how fast Harris could run because he never went all-out in 40-yard timing sessions—again, to avoid injuring his legs. But Steelers running backs coach Dick Hoak once remarked, "I never saw anyone catch him from behind."

He also carved his own special place in NFL legend with his storied Immaculate Reception, a pinball touchdown catch in a 1972 playoff game against the Oakland Raiders. When a desperation pass from Terry Bradshaw, contested by Oakland's Jack Tatum and Pittsburgh's Frenchy Fuqua, caromed backward, Harris made a shoestring catch and ran for the winning score.

Mel Hein . . .

• **Was an All-America at Washington State, where he played all three line positions. He was a member of Washington State's 1930 Rose Bowl team.**

• **Fractured his nose against the Brooklyn Dodgers on the day Pearl Harbor was attacked. He played against the Bears in the NFL title game two weeks later, wearing a mask. "I never lost a tooth playing, and I played against some pretty tough customers," Hein said.**

• **Was selected as the NFL's most valuable player in 1938, almost unheared-of for a lineman.**

• **Was the Giants' captain for 10 years. His jersey, number 7, was retired after his final season in 1945.**

• **Was a supervisor of officials in both the American Football League and National Football League.**

• **Was a charter member of the Pro Football Hall of Fame in 1963.**

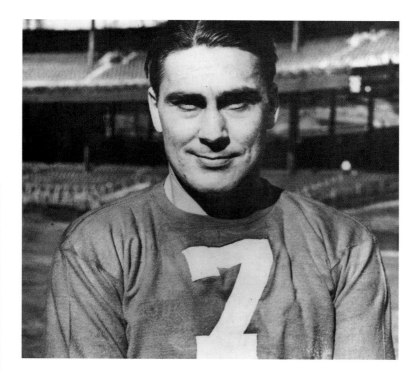

The term "iron man" was synonymous with Mel Hein.

Hein played center and linebacker for the New York Giants for 15 years, from 1931 through 1945, and never missed more than half a game. In fact, he rarely missed a play. Even in his final season, at age 36, he still was playing 60 minutes a game as the highest-paid NFL lineman at $5,000 per season.

Hein won a starting job with the Giants in the second game of his rookie season and became, in the opinion of club owner Wellington Mara, who has seen hundreds of players since the team's birth in 1925, "the number-one player in the first fifty years of the Giants' history."

Hein almost never made it to New York. He was so unnoticed playing at Washington State that he had to write three teams seeking a tryout. When the Providence Steam Roller sent him a contract for $100 per game, he quickly signed and returned it, only to receive an offer from the Giants the next day for $150. So Hein wired the postmaster in Providence, asking him not to deliver the letter he had sent. As it turned out, he spent his entire career in New York.

Hein was a crushing, aggressive blocker whose center duties included a long snap to the tailback on every play. He was chosen all-NFL center eight consecutive seasons, from 1933–1940. In an era when arms, fists, and elbows were used as weapons, he was renowned for his clean play.

Hein excelled on pass defense, rare for a linebacker in those years. He sometimes covered Don Hutson, Green Bay's great end, a task even defensive backs found nearly impossible.

Mel Hein

CENTER

Ted Hendricks . . .

- **Played for the Colts from 1969–1973, for Green Bay in 1974, and for the Raiders from 1975 until his retirement in 1983.**

- **Played on four Super Bowl championship teams, one in Baltimore and three with the Raiders.**

- **Was All-AFC three times with the Colts, four times with the Raiders, and All-NFC in his only season at Green Bay.**

- **Played in eight Pro Bowls.**

- **Didn't like being called "Mad Stork," which originated not only from his angular frame, but also from his penchant for doing goofy things—such as the time he charged onto the field during practice astride a horse.**

- **Was born in Guatemala and was an honors graduate at Miami.**

- **Scored 3 defensive touchdowns and an NFL-record 4 safeties.**

Ted Hendricks

LINEBACKER

Ted Hendricks had an apt nickname: The Mad Stork.

He was nearly 6 feet 8 inches tall and weighed no more than 235 pounds late in his NFL career (he came out of the University of Miami at 215 and played at that weight for several seasons). Bill Curry, a teammate at Baltimore, once described Hendricks as looking "like a series of toothpicks with long, whippy, macaroni arms."

But those arms, with their powerful wrists, could wrap up ball carriers like no other linebacker. They were also long enough to block 25 field goals, extra points, and punts, and intercept 26 passes in 15 seasons with the Colts, Packers, and Raiders. Few players ever were more instinctive. When he played for Raiders defensive coach Charlie Sumner, Hendricks was allowed to line up where he thought he would be the most effective on a given play.

Hendricks was a three-time All-America defensive end at Miami, but pro scouts were wary of his lean frame. "Too frail to be a defensive end in the NFL, too tall to be a linebacker," most of them said. It wasn't until he proved his long arms an advantage in tackling O. J. Simpson time after time in a 1968 game that Baltimore coach Don Shula made him a second-round choice in 1969.

He didn't start until the midpoint of his rookie season in 1969, but, except for the 1975 season, his first year with Oakland, he played year after year at an all-pro level.

The question of Hendricks's durability was answered long before his career ended with a 215-game playing streak . . . and underscored when he was inducted into the Pro Football Hall of Fame in 1990.

Elroy Hirsch . . .

• **Was an All-America football player as a sophomore at Wisconsin in 1942, and again in 1943 as a junior at Michigan, where he had matriculated as part of the Navy's V-12 officer training program.**

• **Was nicknamed "Crazylegs" by Chicago sportswriter Francis Powers, who watched him play for Wisconsin against Great Lakes. "Hirsch ran like a demented duck," Powers wrote. "His crazy legs were gyrating in six different directions all at the same time."**

• **Once placed second in the long jump at a Big Ten track-and-field championship, then pitched a 6-0 shutout for the Wolverines' baseball team on the same afternoon.**

• **Starred in a movie about his life, *Crazylegs—All American*, in 1953.**

• **Caught 387 passes for 7,029 yards and an 18.2-yard average, including his three seasons in the All-America Football Conference.**

• **Caught touchdown passes in 11 consecutive games, including 10 straight during the 1951 season.**

I can't remember Hirsch ever dropping a ball he could get his hands on," said Red Hickey in describing Elroy (Crazylegs) Hirsch, whom he coached when the flanker starred for the Los Angeles Rams.

Hirsch had one of the most remarkable careers in football history. He was an All-America halfback at Wisconsin and Michigan; an all-service running back for the Marines at El Toro Air Station in California; a running back for three seasons with the Chicago Rockets of the All-America Football Conference; and finally, one of the most feared receivers in the NFL.

Hickey, an assistant coach with the Rams, convinced head coach Joe Stydahar to make Hirsch a full-time starter in 1950, the flanker's second season in Los Angeles. It was a brilliant move because Hirsch teamed with receivers Tom Fears, Bob Boyd, and Glenn Davis to give quarterbacks Bob Waterfield and Norm Van Brocklin one of the greatest offenses in NFL history.

In 1951, when the Rams won the NFL championship, Hirsch caught 66 passes for 1,495 yards and a record-tying 17 touchdowns—5 of 70 yards or more. His touchdown mark tied the record of his boyhood idol, Don Hutson, who played in Green Bay, 90 miles southeast of Hirsch's Wausau, Wisconsin, home.

Hirsch perfected the knack of catching a ball over his shoulder—looking it into his hands without turning his body while running at full stride. "That gave him something extra, and made him so great," Hickey said.

"I'm just a busted-down, retreaded halfback who happened to get lucky," Hirsch once said, describing his career.

Cal Hubbard . . .

• **Played for three years at Centenary College in Louisiana and one year at Geneva College in Pennsylvania, where he was an All-America tackle.**

• **Had three offers from NFL teams but followed the advice of his idol, coach Bo McMillan, and chose the New York Giants. "They are sure to pay you," McMillan told him.**

• **Was Green Bay's "policeman," the one player tough enough to keep law and order against unruly opponents.**

• **Finished his career in 1936 by playing for the Giants and Pittsburgh Pirates.**

• **Worked as a baseball umpire in the offseason, and at the end of his NFL career joined the American League and later became its supervisor of umpires.**

• **Is the only person enshrined in both the Baseball Hall of Fame and Pro Football Hall of Fame.**

R obert (Cal) Hubbard was decades ahead of his time. In the mid-twenties, football players who were 6 feet 5 inches and 250 pounds were supposed to be slow. Today, NFL players that size must run 40-yard dashes in less than five seconds.

Athletes weren't timed in the 40 back then, but by all accounts, Hubbard's speed and size would make him a fearsome linebacker in today's game.

Why not? He was fearsome back then.

Hubbard came to the New York Giants in 1927 for $150 per game. For two seasons he played end on offense and linebacker on defense. From that proto-linebacking spot, he filled holes any place along the line of scrimmage. As a rookie, Hubbard helped the Giants' defense limit opponents to just 20 points in 13 games.

The following season, while playing a game in Green Bay, he caught the eye of Packers coach Curly Lambeau, who made no bones about wanting Hubbard to play for his team. Today that is tampering; in that almost-anything-goes era, it was a valid offer. Lambeau's calls underscored Hubbard's desire to leave the hurly-burly of Roaring Twenties New York City for the quiet of Green Bay. "Trade me or I quit," Hubbard told the Giants, so they sent him to Wisconsin.

Lambeau gave him a permanent spot at tackle, and for six seasons, three of which the Packers were NFL champions, Hubbard was an all-pro and the most feared lineman in the league.

Don Hutson . . .

- Was an All-America end at Alabama. The "other" end was future college coaching legend Paul (Bear) Bryant.

- Was delivered to the Packers by the margin of 17 minutes—the difference between the postmarks on two envelopes containing signed contracts. Hutson had second thoughts after signing with the Brooklyn Dodgers, who disdained the pass, so he signed with Green Bay, too. NFL Commissioner Joe Carr ruled that the envelope carrying the earlier post mark would get Hutson's services. The letter to the Packers was postmarked 8:30 A.M., the Dodgers 8:47 A.M. on the same day.

- Led the NFL in scoring with 57 points in 1940, and tied for the lead in interceptions with 6.

- Scored an NFL-record 138 points in 1942, which lasted until 1960 when another Packers player, Paul Hornung, scored 176.

- Intercepted 23 passes in his final four seasons.

- Was NFL most valuable player in 1941 and 1942, and was All-NFL seven times.

O n his first play as an NFL starter, Don Hutson caught an 83-yard touchdown pass from Arnie Herber against the Chicago Bears.

That message reverberated around the league for 11 seasons, from 1935 through 1945, during which Hutson caught 99 touchdown passes and gained 7,991 yards on his 488 receptions— all during an era when most teams passed only 10 or 12 times a game.

Things were different in Green Bay, where first Herber, then Cecil Isbell, made Hutson the most feared weapon in the NFL. For the first time, defenses were forced to double- or triple-cover a receiver, and those who refused were badly burned.

Hutson was 6 feet 1 inch and 180 pounds, and many wondered whether the beanpole could survive the pounding of pro football. But he was a marvelous athlete and a consistent 60-minute player who played safety on defense, placekicked, and never missed a game. He finished his career with a 95-game streak in which he caught at least 1 pass.

Hutson was so good that half a century after he finished playing, he still holds a number of NFL receiving records—eight receiving titles and five in a row; seven years as number one in yardage; nine seasons as the touchdown-reception leader and five in a row.

His best season was 1942 when he set NFL records with 74 catches for 1,211 yards and 17 touchdowns. He was the top scorer five times and, with 138 points in 1942, was the first NFL player to exceed 100 points for a season.

Deacon Jones . . .

• Played for a year at South Carolina State, then at Mississippi Vocational (now Mississippi Valley State), where he was discovered by Rams scouts looking at two players on an opposing team. He was a fourteenth-round pick in 1961.

• Had another nickname with the Rams: "Secretary of Defense."

• Missed just three games during his career.

• Once proclaimed: "I'm the best defensive end around. I'd sure hate to have to play against me."

• Always credited Rams offensive tackle Charlie Cowan with helping him perfect his game. "He was the best I ever faced," Jones said of Cowan, "and I faced him every day in practice. He helped me develop the head slap. Every day after practice, we'd work a half-hour on that move."

• Was all-pro for five consecutive seasons from 1965–1969 and played in eight Pro Bowls. After the 1970 season, he was a member of the NFC squad; two years later, after being traded to the Chargers, he played for the AFC.

D eacon Jones invented the term "sack," then perfected the practice during 14 seasons as a defensive end with the Los Angeles Rams, San Diego Chargers, and Washington Redskins.

The NFL didn't keep an official count of quarterback sacks when Jones played from 1961–1974, but by most counts, he would have etched his place among the most prolific pass rushers in NFL history. As a member of the Rams' famed "Fearsome Foursome" defensive line, Jones shared headlines with Merlin Olsen, Lamar Lundy, and Rosey Grier (later Roger Brown).

Jones perfected the head slap, since banned, to get a jump on pass blockers. It was a crashing hand to the earhole of an offensive lineman's helmet, designed to throw him off balance for just a split second—and that's all Deacon needed to get after a quarterback.

One of the game's most flamboyant players, Jones truly had a love affair with the game. When he returned his first questionnaire to the Rams, he wrote "Deacon" in place of his given name, David. "I picked it out because it had a religous connotation and it would be remembered in the violent world of pro football," he said.

Jones attracted immediate attention with his robust sideline-to-sideline play. "Mobility is what makes a football player exciting," he said, "so I made myself as exciting as hell."

He chased down the fastest players, once catching flanker Bobby Mitchell after running with him for 10 yards before knocking him out of bounds. "I wanted to see if I was as fast as he was," Jones said later.

For 10 yards, at least, he was.

Jack Lambert . . .

• Was a defensive end for two years at Kent State before he was switched to linebacker.

• Weighed just 202 pounds in college, which concerned the Steelers before they made him a second-round draft pick. "We knew Jack was undersized but there was no question he was a football player," personnel director Dick Haley said at the time. "He had the intensity and the instincts to play somewhere."

• Lambert became a starter in the first preseason game of his rookie year.

• Missed just seven games during the first 10 years of his career.

• Was all-pro seven times in nine years and played in nine straight Pro Bowls.

• Was Associated Press NFL defensive player of the year in 1976.

• Was enshrined in the Hall of Fame in 1990.

Jack Lambert

Not surprisingly, Jack Lambert's idol when he was playing middle linebacker at Kent State University was Dick Butkus.

For most of 11 seasons with the Pittsburgh Steelers, the 6-foot 4-inch, 220-pound Lambert was a reflection of Butkus. He also was one of the keys to the Steel Curtain defense, which led the Steelers to four Super Bowl titles in his first six seasons.

Lambert's on-field image was compelling—the gap-toothed snarl, the visible intensity as he itched to get into action, and especially the collisions with blockers and ball carriers. He reminded many of Ray Nitschke, Green Bay's great middle linebacker of the 1960s.

Butkus and Nitschke would seem to be pretty good company, but Lambert saw it differently. "I try to get to the football as opposed to the Butkus and Nitschke types who stood in the middle and dared you to knock them down," he said.

Steelers Pro Football Hall-of-Fame linebacker Jack Ham, who played next to Lambert for most of his career, said the difference with Lambert was his ability on pass defense: "He was as good as they were against the run and dramatically better against the pass."

Lambert, whose quickness gave him the ability to avoid blockers and get to running backs, intercepted 28 passes and probably created many more for his secondary by forcing quarterbacks to throw over his lanky frame.

It was left to Dan Rooney, the son of Steelers founder Art Rooney, Sr., to encapsule the middle linebacker's career: "Jack Lambert demanded total effort from everybody in the organization. He took us to greatness. He was the symbol of our success in the 1970s."

Night Train Lane . . .

• **Got his nickname from Ben Sheets, a teammate with the Rams. Lane spent a lot of time during his rookie training camp learning techniques from all-pro end Tom Fears, who constantly played the song "Night Train" on his phonograph. Sheets walked into Fears's room one day, saw Lane with the song blaring in the background, and said, "Hey, there's 'Night Train.'"**

• **Caught 18 touchdown passes in 1951 while playing with a service team, and though he couldn't compete with the great Rams' receiving corps, he had one fling while playing for the Cardinals—a 98-yard touchdown pass from Ogden Compton against Green Bay in 1953.**

• **Led the NFL in interceptions with 14 in 1952 and 10 in 1954.**

• **Returned 5 interceptions for touchdowns, with 2 of them—80 yards against Green Bay and 42 against Pittsburgh—coming in his rookie season.**

• **Was All-NFL four times with Detroit and once with the Cardinals, and was voted to seven Pro Bowls.**

F ew Hall-of-Fame players came into the NFL with a more humble beginning than Dick (Night Train) Lane. Lane's previous football experience consisted of just one season at Scottsbluff Junior College in Nebraska and four years of service football—and that primarily as a wide receiver. Rams head coach Joe Stydahar signed him with nothing to go on except a scrapbook of tattered newspaper clippings.

For 14 seasons in the NFL, however, Lane wrote the book on how to play cornerback in a new era of pass-and-catch football. His 68 interceptions rank third behind Paul Krause and Emlen Tunnell, but his 14 as a rookie with the Los Angeles Rams have never been surpassed.

"The Train" was bigger—6 feet 2 inches, 210 pounds—than most of the receivers he covered, and he manhandled them as much as possible. Lane excelled in the predominant man-for-man coverage of that time because of his speed, agility, determination, and, as he once said, "a short memory of what happened on the last play."

Lane spent two seasons with the Rams (1952–53), then was acquired by the Chicago Cardinals and Stydahar, who took over as the Cardinals' coach in 1953. Lane spent six years with Chicago, then gained his greatest fame with the Detroit Lions' stiff defensive teams of the early 1960s. By then, he had a reputation as a gambler in coverage.

"Sure, he may get burned once in a while," Lions middle linebacker Joe Schmidt once said, "but he comes up with the big play a lot of times, too. I'd say percentage-wise, he's way ahead of the game."

Night Train Lane

CORNERBACK

Steve Largent . . .

• Caught 136 passes for 2,385 yards and 32 touchdowns at Tulsa University, where one of his coaches was Jerry Rhome, later his offensive coordinator at Seattle and the person responsible for getting him from Houston in a trade.

• Was a fourth-round selection of the Oilers in 1976 after leading the nation's collegiate receivers with 14 touchdowns in both the 1974 and 1975 seasons.

• Teamed with quarterback Jim Zorn for seven seasons, then with Dave Krieg for seven. Largent was the favorite target of both passers.

• Became Seattle's first Pro Bowl player in 1978 and was named to the AFC squad six more times.

• Led the AFC in catches with 71 in 1978; and the NFL in receiving yardage with 1,237 in 1979 and 1,287 in 1985.

• Caught his record-setting 100th touchdown pass at Cincinnati in 1989.

A ll-pro cornerback Mike Haynes of the Los Angeles Raiders said it best about Steve Largent: "For a guy too slow and too short, you sure fooled a lot of people."

For 14 seasons with the Seattle Seahawks, Largent defied all of the projections by which NFL personnel people evaluate players. He ranks second among NFL receivers in catches (819), yardage (13,089), and touchdowns (100). When he retired in 1989, he was first in all three categories.

Not bad for a guy who almost was cut by the Houston Oilers in 1976. The Oilers felt good getting an eighth-round choice for him from the expansion Seahawks.

Largent's speed never demanded double-coverage, yet he was the one receiver defenses circled every time they played against Seattle. "I never felt I knew it all," the 5-foot 11-inch, 191-pound wide receiver said when asked why he was so successful. Largent was a tireless worker and a meticulous pattern runner who was just "fast enough" to post ten 50-catch seasons and eight 1,000-yard seasons, both NFL records. He retired after the 1989 season with an NFL-record streak of 177 games in which he caught at least one pass.

When Largent was honored in Seattle by one of the many charities for which he has toiled tirelessly, former President Ronald Reagan sent a videotaped message: "Several times when I've watched you, I wanted to shout, 'Win one for the Gipper!' You are truly a role model for the rest of us."

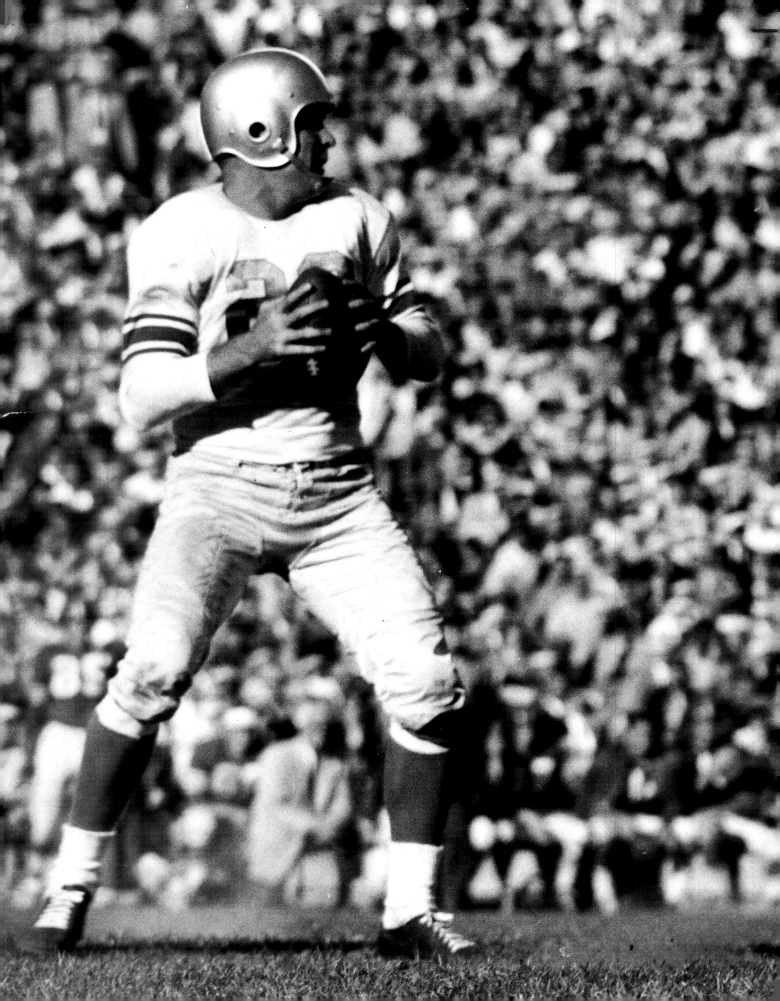

Bobby Layne . . .

- **Was an All-America at the University of Texas in 1947–48, when one of his backfield mates was eventual Dallas Cowboys Hall-of-Fame coach Tom Landry.**

- **Won 26 straight games as a baseball pitcher for Texas.**

- **Had a talented childhood friend: Doak Walker, the Southern Methodist star who became a Hall-of-Fame halfback with the Lions.**

- **Was traded to the Pittsburgh Steelers in 1958, rejoining his old coach, Buddy Parker, and helping the team to its first back-to-back winning seasons.**

- **Always maintained he needed just five hours sleep, and that he was more effective going to bed late; otherwise, he would get up too early and spend all morning mulling over the upcoming game. The latter happened before the Lions lost 56-10 to Cleveland for the 1954 NFL title.**

- **Once kicked 58 consecutive extra points. He led the NFL in scoring with 99 points in 1956, hitting 12 of 15 field goals.**

- **Was inducted into the Hall of Fame in 1967.**

Those people who are audacious enough to claim that Bobby Layne played his greatest games in the dim lights of a friendly saloon never played against him on the football field.

Granted, few had more fun away from football than Layne, but there never was a more feared quarterback with a game on the line. "He is the best third-down quarterback in the game," Paul Brown once said of the man who beat his Cleveland Browns for NFL championships in 1952 and 1953.

Layne never had great statistics (he completed fewer than 50 percent of his passes during 15 NFL seasons with four teams). He is in the Pro Football Hall of Fame because he helped produce three NFL titles with the Detroit Lions, and along the way produced dozens of amazing victories.

In the 1953 NFL Championship Game, the Lions, trailing the Browns 16-10 with 4:10 to play, had the ball on their 20-yard line. Layne told his team in the huddle, "Just give me time, boys . . . dammit, just block."

They did . . . and he hit 4 of 6 passes for 77 yards, including a 33-yard touchdown pass to end Jim Doran with 2:08 to play. The Lions won the game—and the title—17-16.

"Bobby Layne never lost a game in his life," his good friend and teammate, Doak Walker, once said. "Time just ran out on him."

Layne was a tough, hard-nosed player who was one of the last to don a protective mask. He completed 1,814 of 3,700 passes for 26,768 yards and 196 touchdowns, all of which were NFL records when he retired after the 1962 season.

Bob Lilly . . .

• Was the Cowboys' first draft choice; their first all-pro selection (seven times); their first Pro Bowl pick (11 times); the first to be elected to their Ring of Honor at Texas Stadium; and the first to be enshrined in the Hall of Fame (1980).

• Scored 4 touchdowns, 3 on fumble recoveries and 1 on a 17-yard interception return.

• Was the most durable player in Cowboys history. He played in all 196 regular-season games during his 14 seasons.

• Is remembered for hurling his helmet some 40 yards downfield after the Cowboys lost Super Bowl V to Baltimore on a last-second field goal by Jim O'Brien. "I darn near broke my finger and didn't even remember throwing it until one of the Colts retrieved it and handed it to me," Lilly said.

• Always credited his father, Buster, who was wheelchair bound from a motorbike accident suffered when he was 17, with shaping his career: "We worked together every day, even though he couldn't run . . . and he went to every home game I played from high school to 1970, the year we went to our first Super Bowl."

Bob Lilly

DEFENSIVE TACKLE

"A man like this comes along once in a generation, and there won't be another Bob Lilly in my time."

Tom Landry never could be accused of hyperbole, so that judgment, uttered while his defensive tackle still was playing for the Dallas Cowboys, was the ultimate compliment.

Lilly, at 6 feet 5 inches and 262 pounds, was, in the opinion of many long-time observers, the greatest defensive tackle in NFL history. He was lightning quick and he fought double- and triple-teams throughout most of his 14-season career. It didn't matter because, as line coach Ernie Stautner once said, "People who play against him try to get set for his quickness and think they know what to expect. But most of the time he is by them and into the backfield before they get off the dime."

This never was more apparent than in Super Bowl VI, when Lilly chased—and sacked—Miami quarterback Bob Griese for a 29-yard loss that swung the game. Lilly, who grew up in Throckmorton, Texas, was an All-America defensive end at Texas Christian University, and he was the rock of Dallas's famed "Doomsday Defense," which helped the Cowboys to eight consecutive playoff appearances and one Super Bowl victory.

He played defensive end with so-so results until Landry switched him to tackle midway through the 1963 season. Lilly was all-pro for all but one season in the next eight (1964–69, 1971).

Stautner, a Pro Football Hall-of-Fame defensive tackle, put his pupil in sharp focus: "I didn't consider myself in Lilly's class. He could do things I could never do."

Howie Long . . .

• **Was a four-year letterman at Villanova.**

• **Was a second-round draft pick of the Oakland Raiders in 1981.**

• **Was a Northern Collegiate heavyweight boxing champion while in college.**

• **Was named most valuable player of the 1980 Blue-Gray Game, catching the attention of every NFL scout.**

• **Had his best sack year (13) in 1983.**

• **Had 2 career interceptions. He returned one of them 73 yards—but was caught before reaching the end zone.**

Defensive end Howie Long didn't seem to fit the public persona of the Raiders' black-eyepatch mystique when he joined the team in 1981. He smiled a lot, flashing a set of gleaming white teeth that seemed made for Hollywood; he was clean-cut; and his head was topped by a dead-even crew cut that gave him the appearance of a 1950s throwback.

But Long adjusted to the Raiders' mold when he lined up. He was 6 feet 5 inches and 275 pounds, and he coupled his size with ferocity, cat like quickness, and rugged upper-body strength to explode into offensive linemen. When he retired after the 1993 season, his official sack total exceeded 80, and had the league kept those statistics in his rookie 1981 season, it likely would had exceeded 90.

Long became a starter during training camp in 1982. In 1983 he became just the second Raiders defensive lineman named to the Pro Bowl—one of six in which he would play. He once played 81 consecutive games, and he wound up as the last of the Los Angeles Raiders to have played in Oakland. He was selected NFL Defensive Lineman of the Year by the NFL Alumni Association in 1984, and by a nationwide vote of fans in 1986.

Long was the Raiders' defensive star in the 1983 championship season that ended with a victory over Washington in Super Bowl XVIII. When the two teams met during that regular season, he sacked Washington quarterbacks 5 times, his top one-game total.

And he flashed those gleaming white teeth after every one of them.

Ronnie Lott . . .

• Was a two-time All-America at USC, where he ranked second nationally (first in the Pac-10) with 8 interceptions in his senior year.

• Was a reserve guard for USC's basketball team.

• Returned 7 kickoffs for the 49ers as a rookie.

• Was chosen NFL Defensive Back of the Year by the NFL Alumni Association in 1984.

• Had 9 interceptions, including 2 for touchdowns, in 20 postseason games.

• Held or shared the 49ers' interception lead four times.

• Joined Dallas's Mel Renfro and Oakland's Dave Grayson as the only players ever to make the Pro Bowl as both a cornerback and safety.

O uch!" is a common reaction to watching Ronnie Lott flatten a pass receiver.

Lott was one of the best all-around defensive backs during the 1980s, when he led the San Francisco 49ers' defense, which helped the club win a record-tying four Super Bowls.

Lott, who also played for the Los Angeles Raiders and New York Jets, was renowned for his hard-nosed approach to the game. No defensive back ever tackled harder, and he went after anyone who crossed his path—even if that player didn't have the ball.

Lott once said that at the moment of contact, his world went silent and he didn't even hear his victim react. "That's because he knocked the wind out of each of them," said former Cowboys defensive back Dennis Thurman.

Lott played for the Raiders in 1991 and 1992, leading the NFL with 8 interceptions in '91 and the Raiders with 103 tackles in '92. He was set to begin his second season with the New York Jets in 1994.

A first-round draft choice from the University of Southern California in 1981, Lott exploded onto the NFL scene, setting a rookie record by returning 3 of his 7 interceptions for touchdowns. He played cornerback for four seasons—and went to the Pro Bowl after each one—then moved to free safety. In 1986, he led the NFL with 10 interceptions, his top season in that respect.

And he never stopped hitting.

CORNERBACK-SAFETY

Sid Luckman . . .

• Came to the Bears when they acquired the Pittsburgh Steelers' number-one draft choice in 1939.

• Was all-pro six times between 1941 and 1947, and was the NFL's most valuable player in 1943.

• Led the Bears to four NFL titles and six second-place finishes.

• Was a fine multipurpose player with the Bears. He had 17 interceptions as a defensive back, and he punted 230 times for a 38.4-yard average. Threw 28 touchdown passes in 1943.

• Turned down a $25,000 offer in 1946 to become player-coach of the Chicago Rockets of the new All-America Football Conference, saying, "How could I quit a club that had done so much for me?"

Sid Luckman was more than a great passer, he was a football pioneer. Luckman, the league's first successful T-formation quarterback, helped to revolutionize the game at every level.

He was a "triple-threat" tailback at Columbia University in Manhattan when the Chicago Bears drafted him on the first round in 1939. The offenses of choice at that time were the various wingback formations. The "T" was a dusty footnote from the turn of the century, when it had been popularized by Amos Alonzo Stagg at the University of Chicago.

As Luckman prepared to play in the 1939 College All-Star Game, Bears coach George Halas handed him a new playbook that featured nothing but T-formation plays. Luckman, who was a better runner than passer in college, had never even seen the system before. When he joined the Bears, he struggled so badly that Halas moved him to running back for a short time before giving him a second chance.

Luckman soon became a master T-formation quarterback, with his dazzling ball handling and canny play-calling. He became a fine passer, throwing for 14,683 yards and 137 touchdowns during his 12-year career with Chicago. His most famous game was the 73-0 rout of the Washington Redskins in the 1940 NFL Championship Game. Ironically, he threw just 1 touchdown pass that day, but the impact of the win popularized the T for good. Luckman tagged the Redskins again with a 5-touchdown, 286-yard performance in the 1943 title game.

Earlier in 1943, he became the first player to throw 7 touchdown passes in a game, against the New York Giants. Appropriately, that performance fell on Sid Luckman Day at New York's Polo Grounds.

Sid Luckman

QUARTERBACK

Gino Marchetti . . .

• Was a member of the University of San Francisco's unbeaten 1950 team that sent 10 starters into the NFL, not to mention head coach Joe Kuharich and the school's publicist— Commissioner-to-be Pete Rozelle.

• Retired after serving as player-coach in 1963, then came back to play with the Colts' 1964 Western Division championship team. And when injuries overwhelmed Baltimore's defensive line in 1966, he came back again to play four games.

• Made the biggest defensive play for the Colts when they won the 1958 NFL Championship Game against the Giants, stopping Frank Gifford on a key third-down play late in the fourth quarter. Marchetti broke his ankle on that play when Big Daddy Lipscomb fell on his leg, but he stayed on the sidelines long enough to watch his team tie the game with seven seconds left to play.

• Played in 10 Pro Bowls in 11 years, from 1955–1965.

• Was inducted into the Hall of Fame in 1972— in the same class as his college teammate, halfback Ollie Matson.

Great NFL careers happen in a variety of ways, and never without a bit of luck. Consider Gino Marchetti, who in the NFL's Golden Anniversary season of 1969 was voted the "greatest defensive end in NFL history."

Marchetti survived fighting in Europe during World War II; he was an "add-on" when a scout from Compton Junior College invited his brother to play football at the school; and he survived a year with probably the worst team in NFL history—the 1952 Dallas Texans—and another year at offensive tackle with the Baltimore Colts that almost drove him to the Canadian Football League.

Fortunately, Weeb Ewbank came along and made him a defensive end in 1954.

Marchetti played 13 seasons with the Colts, and no one ever rushed the passer better. Two-way tackle Leo Nomellini, the San Francisco 49ers great who played against Baltimore twice a year, said, "He had the look of death in his eyes on the field. There was no way to keep him off the passer or ball carrier. He knocked down blockers like they were rag dolls. It's just a good thing his parents brought him up right."

"Quickness and concentration were the big things I had going for me," Marchetti said. "I'd always line up so I could see the tackle in front of me, plus the guard and center. The moment any of those three moved a muscle, I was gone.

"The guy in front of me had to be just as quick because if I got that split-second jump and got my hands on his shoulders, he was finished. I don't know how or why I did some of those things."

Dan Marino . . .

• Led the University of Pittsburgh to a 42-6 record in four seasons, including a pair of number-two rankings.

• Broke the single-season record of 36 touchdown passes, shared by Y. A. Tittle and George Blanda, by a whopping 12 in 1984.

• Has had only 1 of every 32 passes intercepted during his career, and has been sacked just once per 38 attempts.

• Had the third-best single-game passing performance in NFL history with 521 yards against the Jets in 1988.

• Reached 30,000 passing yards in 114 games, fastest in NFL history, in 1990; topped 40,000 in 153 games, also fastest ever, in 1993.

• Was the fourth-round pick of the Kansas City Royals in the 1979 amateur draft after a fine high school pitching career.

• Was the USFL's first overall draft pick in 1983, by the Los Angeles Express.

Dan Marino no doubt will own most of the NFL passing records when he finally retires, but consider some that he already has:

    Most yards, season: 5,084 in 1984.

    Most touchdown passes, season: 48 in 1984.

Most games, career, 400+ yards passing: 10.

Most seasons, 4,000+ yards passing: 4.

Marino, who missed the last 11 games of the 1993 season with an Achilles tendon injury, has four key ingredients that make him a great quarterback: great peripheral vision, which allows him to see pass rushers closing in; a quick release to keep him from being sacked; a strong arm; and great poise in the pocket, which enables the other three qualities to work.

Marino became the Miami Dolphins' starting quarterback in the sixth game of his rookie season in 1983. He soon became the first rookie quarterback to lead the AFC in passing since the NFL-AFL merger in 1970, and the first voted as a Pro Bowl starter.

A year later, while leading the Dolphins to Super Bowl XIX, he was a unanimous pick as the league's most valuable player after shattering records for yards and touchdowns. He had a record-setting four games with 400 or more yards, and 12 games with 3 or more touchdown passes.

Marino was chosen by the Dolphins with the twenty-seventh overall pick of the 1983 draft. Twenty-six players were selected before Marino, including five quarterbacks. To this day, there are many NFL personnel departments that consider it one of the worst blunders they ever made.

Hugh McElhenny . . .

• Set a Pacific Coast Conference rushing mark of 2,499 yards at the University of Washington from 1949–1951.

• Received high praise from 49ers general manager Lou Spadia: "When Hugh joined the 49ers in 1952, it was questionable whether our franchise could survive. McElhenny removed all doubts. That's why we call him our franchise saver."

• Was picked by the expansion Minnesota Vikings in 1961. Two years later he was a member of the New York Giants' 1963 Eastern Division champions, with whom he played in his only NFL title game. He finished his career with Detroit in 1964.

• Caught 264 passes for 3,247 yards and 20 touchdowns. He twice caught 37 passes, in 1957 and 1961.

• Returned 126 punts for 920 yards and 2 touchdowns and averaged 23.1 yards on 83 kickoff returns.

• Was inducted into the Pro Football Hall of Fame in 1970, his first year of eligibility.

T he King," as 6-foot 1-inch, 198-pound Hugh McElhenny was known, ruled the NFL for 13 seasons and performed athletic feats rarely seen before or since.

McElhenny's official statistics say he gained 5,281 rushing yards, but anyone who played with him, coached him, or chased him claims he is the greatest open-field runner in NFL history. McElhenny spiced his runs with sudden bursts of blinding speed, changes of pace, fakes, sidesteps, and other trademarks of his electrifying style. In a playoff game against Detroit in 1957, he caught a pass from quarterback Y. A. Tittle and ran 47 yards for a touchdown . . . officially. The films later showed that he actually ran about 100 yards as he weaved back and forth across the field en route to the end zone.

McElhenny, was a first-round draft choice of the 49ers in 1952. When that season ended, he had recorded the NFL's longest run, 89 yards, and its longest punt return, 94 yards; compiled its top rushing average, 7.0 yards per carry; scored 2 touchdowns in the first of his six Pro Bowl appearances; and was everybody's choice for rookie of the year.

McElhenny's running style was just as feared when he was catching the ball or returning punts and kickoffs. More than half of his combined 11,369 yards were from those three duties, and he scored 22 of his 60 career touchdowns on passes and punt returns.

With all that he achieved during his nine seasons with the 49ers, McElhenny often said his finest season, "taking everything into account," was in 1961, when he rang up 1,197 all-purpose yards after being selected by the Minnesota Vikings in the expansion draft.

Joe Montana . . .

• Set an NFL record with five consecutive 300-yard passing games in the strike-shortened 1982 season.

• Led Notre Dame to the 1977 national championship as a junior; in his senior year, he capped a 22-point fourth-quarter comeback with the winning touchdown pass on the last play of the Cotton Bowl for a 35-34 victory over Houston.

• Was voted to eight Pro Bowls, including one with the Chiefs.

• Has thrown for more than 5,000 passing yards and 42 touchdowns in the postseason.

• Started 14 games, including three playoff contests, with the Chiefs in his first season in Kansas City in 1993.

• Had his best statistical game—476 yards and 6 touchdown passes—against Atlanta in 1990.

• Beat the Bengals in Super Bowls XVI and XXIII; he also downed Miami in Super Bowl XIX and Denver in Super Bowl XXIV. Montana was MVP in three of those games.

Some people think Joe Montana is the finest quarterback in NFL history. If accomplishments and personal testimonials mean anything, they may be correct.

Montana led the San Francisco 49ers to four Super Bowl titles, and over 14 seasons with the 49ers and one with the Kansas City Chiefs, he is the NFL's highest-rated passer. He entered the 1994 season with a career rating of 93.1.

Montana, a third-round draft pick of the 49ers in 1979, brought a reputation from Notre Dame as the master of the comeback, and he kept it going in the NFL. So far, he has rallied the 49ers and Chiefs from fourth-quarter deficits to victory 29 times.

No comeback was more dramatic than the touchdown pass to wide receiver Dwight Clark in the final minute of the 1981 NFC title game against Dallas that sent the 49ers to their first Super Bowl; or Montana's improbable 92-yard drive in the final three minutes of Super Bowl XXIII against the Cincinnati Bengals, a march he finished with a winning touchdown pass to John Taylor with 34 seconds to play.

Montana does not have an overpowering arm, but he was the perfect quarterback for coach Bill Walsh's complex offense in San Francisco. Montana works with the same system in Kansas City. He has led the NFC in passing five times, and in touchdown passes four times. He also eaned NFL most valuable player honors three times.

Through it all, he has completed more than 3,100 passes for better than 37,000 yards and more than 250 touchdowns.

Those numbers are as hard to beat as Joe Montana in a Super Bowl.

Marion Motley . . .

• **Was the catalyst in one of Paul Brown's most famous innovations—the draw play.** Quarterback Otto Graham, panicked by a heavy pass rush, slipped the ball to Motley, who was trying to protect him. The fullback ran for a big gain. When Brown saw the play on film, he added a more deliberate version to his offense.

• **Gained 188 yards on 11 carries against Pittsburgh in 1950.** That 17.09-yard average still is an NFL record.

• **Played eight full seasons for the Browns, and briefly for Pittsburgh in 1955.** He rushed for 4,720 yards and 31 touchdowns and caught 85 passes for 1,107 and 7 scores.

• **Got heavy duty as a kickoff returner during the Browns' AAFC years, averaging more than 23 yards per return.**

• **Played on five league championship teams with the Browns, four in the AAFC and one in the NFL.**

• **Led the Browns in rushing once and was the AAFC's career leader during that league's four-year existence; also led the league in his first NFL season in 1950.**

Marion Motley was pro football's best-kept secret until Paul Brown unleashed him on the All-America Football Conference in 1946. Motley then became the sport's greatest fullback—as runner and blocker—for the next eight seasons in the AAFC and NFL. He compiled a 5.7-yard rushing average in those two leagues.

Motley also was a great linebacker. Brown, who coached him during those seasons, said he could have made the Pro Football Hall of Fame at that position alone.

Motley weighed 238 pounds, and, Brown noted, "when he ran off tackle, players seemed to fly off him in all directions . . . and he could run away from linebackers and defensive backs, if he didn't trample them first."

Brown knew. In high school, Motley had played against Massillon, coached by Brown, and later played for Brown at Great Lakes Naval Training Center in 1945.

Brown established his AAFC team in Cleveland the following year and, in a historic move, he invited Motley and lineman Bill Willis, who had played for Brown at Ohio State, to join the team. They were the first African-Americans in pro football since the 1930s. Both are in the Pro Football Hall of Fame.

"No other team was interested in Marion because he hadn't played long enough in college or the service to attract any attention," Brown wrote in his autobiography, *PB: The Paul Brown Story*. "But he became our greatest fullback ever. And no one ever cared more about his team and whether it won or lost."

Anthony Muñoz . . .

• **Was named to 11 Pro Bowls and played in nine.**

• **Was named Offensive Lineman of the Year three times by the NFL Alumni Association, and four times by his peers in the NFL Players Association.**

• **Missed just one start—in 1983 because of an ankle injury—in the 185 games he played. He entered that game on the second series and played the rest of the way.**

• **Caught 4 touchdown passes on tackle-eligible plays, including 2 in 1986.**

• **Allowed just 1½ sacks in 1986 and was the only unanimous selection to the Pro Bowl that season.**

No one pays money to see offensive linemen, but for 13 seasons in Cincinnati, watching offensive tackle Anthony Muñoz, one of the greatest offensive linemen in NFL history, was worth the price of admission.

That's not bad for a guy who appeared to be a colossal gamble when the Cincinnati Bengals made him their number-one draft choice in 1980. Muñoz had suffered three serious knee injuries while playing at the University of Southern California, but when Bengals general manager Paul Brown watched the tackle's flawless performance in the 1980 Rose Bowl, he made up his mind to draft him.

Muñoz, at 6 feet 6 inches and 285 pounds, was among the NFL's biggest linemen when he joined the Bengals in 1980. Yet he had surprising athletic grace, which combined with his tremendous foot quickness and strength to make him a premier pass protector at the crucial left tackle spot, which protects the blind side of a right-handed quarterback.

"He had such outstanding agility and quickness, he could have been a linebacker or tight end," said his line coach, Jim McNally.

Muñoz, easygoing and affable away from the game but dedicated and intense on the field, made pass blocking seem casual, almost fun, as he smothered the rushes of some of the NFL's best defensive ends and linebackers.

No one worked harder. Muñoz installed a set of weight equipment in the basement of his home and worked year-round to stay in peak condition, which allowed him to play in 177 consecutive nonstrike games at one point in his career.

Anthony Muñoz

TACKLE

Bronko Nagurski . . .

• Was an All-America tackle *and* fullback at the University of Minnesota in 1929–1930.

• Teamed with Red Grange for several years in Chicago—a "Dream Backfield" that featured two of college football's greatest legends.

• Was all-pro in 1932–34.

• Knew how to make an impression. Clarke Hinkle, an all-pro with the Packers, on the first time he tackled Nagurski: "I had to have five stitches in my face. My biggest thrill in football was the day he announced his retirement."

• Was largely responsible for a major rules change. In the Bears' 9-0 victory over Portsmouth for the 1932 NFL title, Nagurski threw a pass for the game's only touchdown. Portsmouth protested that he wasn't the required five yards behind the line of scrimmage when he threw the ball, and the NFL altered the rule a year later to eliminate distance judgments.

• Was a charter enshrinee of the Pro Football Hall of Fame in 1963.

Bronko Nagurski

B ronko Nagurski still symbolizes the powerful football player. The 6-foot 2-inch, 230-pound Minnesotan, with the size-19 collar and size 19½ ring finger, was larger than life when he dominated football fields in the 1930s.

Nagurski became a physical wonder in the minds of the nation during two All-America seasons at the University of Minnesota and eight as a fullback and linebacker with the Chicago Bears—plus a one-year second tour with Chicago as running back and tackle at age 35, six years after he had retired.

Nagurski never was as big as people imagined, but he certainly was as good as advertised. He was barrel-chested, and his legs looked like tree trunks. When he blasted into tacklers, he left a wake of tangled bodies.

"When you hit him at the ankles, it was like getting an electric shock," Bears teammate Red Grange once said. "If you hit him above the ankles, you were apt to get killed."

Nagurski helped the Bears to NFL titles in 1932 and 1933. He retired after the 1937 season when Bears owner-coach George Halas refused his demand for a $6,000 salary, and he became one of the nation's most popular pro wrestlers.

When World War II sapped Chicago's roster, the Bears asked Nagurski to return for the 1943 season. Though he had been away from football for six years, Nagurski played tackle and did some occasional running, forging a major role in leading the Bears to another NFL championship. His touchdown run against the Redskins gave Chicago the lead for good in its 41-21 victory in the 1943 title game.

FULLBACK

To Olaf Haugsrud the true
friend and representative of
Norse meet. Very sincerely
"Ernie" N...

FULLBACK

Ernie Nevers . . .

• Compared favorably to Jim Thorpe, according to Pop Warner, who coached them both: "Nevers was better than Thorpe. He had more desire and determination, and he could do a lot of things that Thorpe couldn't do."

• "Just did it" long before Bo Jackson & Deion Sanders. In 1926, Nevers signed with the Duluth Eskimos of the NFL and with the Browns of the American League with a proviso that he could leave the baseball team in September if it were not in pennant contention.

• Had a 6-12 lifetime pitching record with the Browns, and gave up 1 of Babe Ruth's record 60 home runs in 1927.

• Got his first major-league hit off fabled Walter Johnson. After getting two strikes, Johnson told Nevers the next pitch was coming right down the middle, and he smacked it for a double. "Johnson was just trying to make me look good," Nevers said later.

The Roaring '20s produced some of America's most fabled college and professional sports heroes, and fullback Ernie Nevers was near the top of the list. Nevers, a man with Hollywood looks, played professional football, baseball, and basketball.

At 6 feet and 205 pounds, he was a great football player who ran, passed, punted, kicked, and always was his team's best defensive player in college and the NFL. He was a two-time All-America running back at Stanford under coach Glenn (Pop) Warner. Nevers gained national acclaim by outperforming Notre Dame's famed Four Horsemen in the 1926 Rose Bowl, though his team lost 27-10.

A star pitcher (as well as a track star) for Stanford, he signed a contract with the St. Louis Browns and pitched for three years. In 1926, Ole Haugsrud, a young man with great dreams who had attended the same Superior, Wisconsin, high school as Nevers, signed him to a contract with the Duluth Eskimos, giving the NFL a much-needed star to counter Red Grange's new American Football League.

The Duluth team soon became known as "Ernie Nevers's Traveling Eskimos." They played 14 NFL games and 15 exhibitions in 1926, covering 17,000 miles. The team played five games in one eight-day stretch—with just 13 players.

Nevers played with Duluth for two years, but his best seasons were for the Chicago Cardinals from 1929–1931. (He also coached the Cardinals in 1930.) He still holds the NFL record of 40 points in one game, set against the Bears in 1929.

Ray Nitschke . . .

• **Led Illinois in scoring with 5 touchdowns as a senior. He had a 6.5-yard rushing average for three seasons, though he primarily was used as a blocker.**

• **Listened to his brother's counsel about the importance of a college education and turned down a $3,000 baseball contract from the St. Louis Browns to attend Illinois. "It was the smartest thing I ever did," said Nitschke, an all-state quarterback.**

• **Was rated the NFL's best in the mid-1960s, by a special panel of retired NFL linebackers who used strength, quick reactions, speed, toughness, and leadership as their criteria.**

• **Impressed his peers. Les Richter, a Rams' linebacker for nine seasons, on Nitschke: "It's not so much his speed or even his quickness . . . it's a desire to make the play, an ability to get to the right spot ahead of everybody else."**

• **Had a 42-yard interception return for a touchdown in the 1965 Pro Bowl, his only appearance in the series. He also had 25 career interceptions.**

In the 1960s, Ray Nitschke, in a conservative, dark blue suit and dark-rimmed glasses, seemed more like a friendly neighborhood banker than one of the NFL's most ferocious middle linebackers.

Come game time, it was a different story. Front teeth missing, Nitschke snarled at the offense as he launched himself into plays. He was a savage tackler. "You want them to respect you when they run a play," he once said. "You want them to remember that you are there."

Yet Nitschke had a gentle, sensitive side away from the game. He once took offense when a TV interviewer described him as "an animal" during a postgame session. Packers coach Vince Lombardi, whose fiery tirades singed the toughest of his players, got after Nitschke only in the privacy of his office, lest he crush his linebacker's spirit and render him ineffective.

Nitschke was the core of the great Green Bay defense that helped produce five NFL championships and victories in Super Bowls I and II. He was the first player from the Packers' defense to be inducted into the Pro Football Hall of Fame.

A third-round draft pick in 1958 after three years at Illinois as a fullback-linebacker, Nitschke started eight games as a rookie but didn't get the job for good until midway through the 1960 season, when incumbent Tom Bettis was injured. Nitschke's 1961 season was interrupted by Army duty, but in 1962 he was MVP of the NFL title game with 2 fumble recoveries and a deflected pass as the Packers defeated the Giants 16-7 in minus-20-degree wind-chill conditions.

He loved every moment of it.

Merlin Olsen . . .

• Was a number-one pick from Utah State in 1962, having won the Outland Trophy as college football's outstanding lineman as a senior.

• Was Phi Beta Kappa as an undergrad and later got a master's degree in finance.

• Also was the first pick of the AFL's Denver Broncos in '62.

• Became a starter in the third preseason game of his rookie season.

• Played 198 straight games after missing two late in his first year.

• Became a TV star in the role of Jonathan Garvey in "Little House on the Prairie," and later starred as Father Murphy in the show of that name.

• Had two brothers who also played in the NFL. Phil joined Merlin with the Rams, then moved to the Denver Broncos; Orrin played with the Kansas City Chiefs.

T he New York Giants had just defeated the Los Angeles Rams in a 1962 preseason game when Rams assistant coach Harland Svare, who had played for the Giants, approached his friend Jack Stroud, a three-time Pro Bowl guard for New York. "What did you think of the kid?" Svare asked him. "I figured he'd get a good test from you."

Stroud, exhausted from a long evening spent battling rookie defensive tackle Merlin Olsen, looked at Svare. "Thanks for not doing me a favor," he replied with a wan smile.

That was the consensus among those who played against Olsen. For the first half of his 15-year, Pro Football Hall-of-Fame career with the Rams, he was a member of the famed "Fearsome Foursome" defensive line, along with Deacon Jones, Rosey Grier, Lamar Lundy, and later, Roger Brown.

No end-tackle tandem ever worked better than Olsen and Jones, who also is in the Hall of Fame. "Deacon knew what to expect from me, and I from him," Olsen said. "He was quicker than I, which meant that sometimes he would be leaving some territory uncovered. I accepted the responsibility of covering that territory."

Later in his career, with different defensive philosophy and teammates, Olsen was more freewheeling but no less effective. He was voted to the Pro Bowl 14 consecutive times and named all-pro five straight seasons.

"A good defensive lineman must be part charging buffalo and part ballet dancer," Olsen said. "And he must know when to be which. It's more an emotional state and an ability to concentrate. If you haven't those, you can't generate the horsepower."

Jim Otto . . .

• Built himself up from 205 to 255 pounds in his rookie year, and played at that weight for the rest of his career.

• Originally wore jersey number 50, but a Raiders public relations man, noting the letter "o" at both ends of Otto's name, convinced him to take 00.

• Was the first Raiders player enshrined in the Pro Fooball Hall of Fame.

• Was not drafted by the NFL in 1960, and turned down its overtures to jump during the AFL-NFL war, citing his loyalty toward an organization that had given him a chance to play.

• Played in six AFL/AFC Championship Games, Super Bowl II, and 12 AFL All-Star Games and AFC-NFC Pro Bowls.

It was like a scene from an old movie—the young football player arriving to play for his new team with two pairs of football cleats slung around his neck, his hands carrying two battered suitcases.

That was how Jim Otto arrived to play for the Oakland Raiders in 1960—and he didn't leave for 15 years. Otto started 210 consecutive regular-season games, plus 98 more in the preseason, playoffs, and all-star games.

He was the only all-league center in the 10 years of the American Football League, and following the merger of the AFL and NFL, he was the all-AFC center for three more.

Otto, a 205-pound center and middle linebacker at the University of Miami, was drafted by Minneapolis before that AFL franchise moved to Oakland prior to the AFL's first season. Raiders coach Eddie Erdelatz had been so impressed with Otto's performance as a linebacker against one of his Navy teams that he wanted him to play that position as a pro. Otto, knowing his only injuries had come while playing defense, lagged in defensive practice and was lined up at center.

He was renowned not only for his intelligent play (in one season he made blocking calls at the line of scrimmage on 650 plays and erred on just four), but also for his leadership, dedication, and pride. Otto shrugged off injuries—he had six knee operations—and was the symbol of the Raiders' great record during most of his career.

"He loved to win," said long-time teammate George Blanda. "He led by example, and he set the tempo. He gave the Raiders an image of hard discipline, hard work, and hard-nosed football."

Jim Otto

CENTER

Alan Page . . .

• **Was an All-America defensive end at Notre Dame in 1966.**

• **Was credited with 28 blocked punts and kicks, 23 fumble recoveries, and 2 interceptions during his NFL career.**

• **Became a starter in the fourth week of his rookie year and never missed another game. In all, he played in 237 games, including 218 in the regular season.**

• **Was the second Canton, Ohio, native—Marion Motley was the first—to be inducted into the Hall of Fame.**

• **Played next to end Jim Marshall on the Vikings' "Purple People Eaters" defense, forming perhaps the quickest tandem in NFL history.**

• **Was credited with 1,423 tackles, 1,071 of them solo.**

• **Unofficially led the Bears with 11½ sacks in his first season in Chicago.**

• **Now is a justice on the Minnesota Supreme Court.**

A lan Page was a native of Canton, Ohio, who played high school football at Canton Central Catholic. Twenty-five years after graduating, he returned to his native city to be inducted into the Pro Football Hall of Fame.

The trip to the Hall of Fame took 15 seasons in the NFL and wound through Minnesota and Chicago, where he played right defensive tackle. His career carried him to four Super Bowls, nine Pro Bowls, and a host of postseason games, mostly as a member of the Minnesota Vikings' famed "Purple People Eaters" defensive line, which teamed him with Carl Eller, Jim Marshall, and Gary Larsen.

Page was an incredibly quick tackle, a quality that he always considered more important than his weight. In fact, he weighed 255 pounds when he joined the Vikings as a first-round draft pick from Notre Dame in 1967; each year thereafter, his weight declined, much to the consternation of his coaches.

At any weight, Page was something to behold. He played sideline-to-sideline, and he was so quick that it was nearly impossible to get a full block on him. Sometimes it was hard to tell whether he was offsides or had moved at the exact instant the center flexed his hand to snap the ball.

Page once described his role: "My job is not to sit back and wait and then react to what the offense does. My job is to go after them. If you are going to make a mistake, make it aggressively."

In 1971, he played so aggressively that he was named UPI's NFC player of the year. In his career, he was credited unofficially by the Vikings with 173 sacks.

Walter Payton . . .

• Gained 3,563 yards in four years at Jackson State and set an NCAA scoring record with 464 points on 66 touchdowns, 5 field goals, and 53 extra points.

• Missed one game in his rookie year, then did not miss another (186 consecutive nonstrike games).

• Was named all-pro seven times and voted to the Pro Bowl nine times.

• Completed 11 of 34 passes for 331 yards and 8 touchdowns in his career.

• Competed against his brother Eddie, who returned punts and kickoffs for four NFL teams.

• Led the NFL with a 31.7-yard kickoff-return average during his rookie season but, amazingly, didn't make the all-rookie team.

• Was inducted into the Pro Football Hall of Fame in 1993.

When Chicago Bears general manager Jim Finks drafted Walter Payton in the first round in 1975, he said, "Payton is better than Jim Brown. He is better than O.J. Simpson."

It sounded like hyperbole at the time, but when Payton retired after the 1987 season, the man nicknamed "Sweetness" was the NFL's all-time leading rusher with 16,726 yards, having surpassed Brown's record of 12,312 yards in 1984.

It became just one of many superlatives beside Payton's name in the NFL record book: ten 1,000-yard rushing seasons . . . 77 games with 100 or more rushing yards . . . 21,803 combined yards (including 4,538 on 492 pass receptions) . . . and the single-game mark of 275 yards.

Payton was small at 5 feet 10 inches, 202 pounds. But he was a ferocious competitor who barreled into, over, and through would-be tacklers, getting his yardage a chunk at a time rather than breaking long gainers. Payton had an unusual, straight-legged running style. It accentuated the strength that came from his thighs, hamstrings, and buttocks—muscles made extraordinarily strong by hour upon hour of running up and down a steep railroad embankment near his Mississippi home during the offseason.

Payton's strength propelled him to an NFL-leading 1,852 yards in 1977, his best season and the third best in history at the time, and to four other NFC rushing titles during his first six seasons. Despite the gaudy rushing figures, he took even greater pride in his blocking ability, delighting in his collisions with blitzers.

Maybe "Sweetness" was a misnomer.

Jerry Rice . . .

• Holds the NFL touchdown-reception record with 118 going into the 1994 season.

• Has 708 receptions (fifth all-time) for 11,776 yards (sixth).

• Led the NFL in receiving yardage three times, and in 1990 became fifth player in history to catch 100 passes in a season.

• Won NFL most valuable player honors in 1987, and was voted MVP of Super Bowl XXIII after catching 11 passes for 215 yards.

• Broke the scoring reception mark against Miami in 1992, the same day he became the ninth NFL player to gain 10,000 receiving yards.

• Caught a touchdown pass in an NFL-record 13 consecutive games.

• Accumulated 4,693 receiving yards at Mississippi Valley State, including 1,845 in his senior year. He scored 28 touchdowns that season.

Jerry Rice is modern proof that you need not come from a big school to become a potential Pro Football Hall-of-Fame player in the NFL.

Rice also is heading for the College Football Hall of Fame some day, having set 18 NCAA Division II records as a wide receiver at Mississippi Valley State. Even those prolific numbers didn't convince the NFL teams that bypassed him in the first round of the 1985 NFL draft before the San Francisco 49ers chose him with the sixteenth pick.

It was a match made in heaven—and in the fertile mind of 49ers coach Bill Walsh, who fit Rice neatly into his already productive pass offense. Rice and quarterback Joe Montana became the NFL's top combination, producing more than 7,000 yards and back-to-back Super Bowl victories in XXIII and XXIV.

Steve Young took over as quarterback in 1991, and the beat goes on. Young and Rice have teamed for nearly 4,000 yards so far.

Rice, though 6 feet 2 inches and 200 pounds, looks like a good hit would snap him in two, but there aren't many stronger wide receivers in the NFL. He can outmuscle defensive backs for the ball, and he is a fearless downfield blocker.

"He's the talent you look for to define all the skills," said R.C. Owens, another famous 49ers receiver and master of the "Alley Oop" pass. "He runs the field, pattern-wise, with great precision. He gets off the line. He has three speeds, and changes them at any time. He has great hands. He can react to the ball wherever it is.

"Of all the guys I've watched in more than four decades, Jerry Rice epitomizes what the position is about."

Barry Sanders . . .

• **Established 13 NCAA rushing records at Oklahoma State.**

• **Was named to the Pro Bowl in each of his first five seasons.**

• **Had a club-record eight 100-yard games in 1991.**

• **Led all NFL backs in total rushing yards between 1989 and 1993.**

• **Has earned his yardage. He has played primarily in a Run-and-Shoot offense, where he has no second back or tight end to provide added blocking.**

• **Has a problem with his size—but only when buying clothes. He buys size-36 pants to accommodate his huge thighs, then has the waist taken in.**

B arry Sanders has answered all of the questions about the wisdom of his departure from Oklahoma State with a year of eligibility remaining to play in the NFL.

He is one of the NFL's best running backs, winner of one NFL and two NFC rushing titles in five seasons. And he became the Lions' all-time rusher in just his fourth season.

In 1988, Sanders became one of the few juniors ever to win the Heisman Trophy. But there were many who questioned whether a man of his size (5 feet 8 inches, 203 pounds) could sustain the pounding he would take as an NFL runner. Sanders answered that question in less than a year. He won the NFC rushing title as a rookie with 1,470 yards, becoming Detroit's first rushing champion since Byron (Whizzer) White in 1940. On his first NFL play from scrimmage, after being with the Lions just two days, he burst for 18 yards in the 1989 season opener against Phoenix.

Sanders won the NFL rushing title with 1,304 yards in 1990, and has gained more than 1,000 yards in each of his five seasons. Ironically, his best season was 1991, when he gained 1,548 yards but lost the title by just 15 yards to Emmitt Smith of Dallas.

Sanders has great quickness and change of pace when he runs, giving tacklers little chance to tackle him with full force. "When we played against him the first time, we were all complaining because we thought he had Vaseline on his jersey," said former Pro Bowl defensive tackle Keith Millard of the Vikings. "Really. We'd get our hands on his jersey, and he'd be in and out of our hands like that. We just couldn't believe."

Gale Sayers . . .

• Was known as "The Kansas Comet" during his All-America seasons at the University of Kansas, where he gained 2,675 rushing yards.

• Chose the Bears over the AFL's Kansas City Chiefs, both of which drafted him in the first round in 1965. He was one of Chicago's three first-round choices that season.

• Went through a grueling knee rehabilitation following a 1968 injury, then returned to get his second NFL rushing title with 1,032 yards in 1969.

• Finished his NFL career with 9,435 all-purpose yards, including 4,956 rushing yards in less than five full seasons.

• Was the player of the game in three of four Pro Bowl appearances.

• Is the all-time NFL kickoff-return leader with a 30.6-yard average.

• Was all-pro in each of his five full seasons.

No player had a more dramatic NFL debut than Gale Sayers of the Chicago Bears in 1965. His first-year exploits included a 72-yard punt return, a 93-yard kickoff return, and a 26-yard left-handed touchdown option pass (by a right-handed passer).

The rookie's amazing feats did not end there. He had 4 touchdowns against the Minnesota Vikings, including a 96-yard kickoff return . . . an NFL-record-tying 6 touchdowns (an 80-yard pass reception, 21-, 7-, 50-, and 1-yard runs, and an 85-yard punt return) against the San Francisco 49ers . . . a total of 2,272 combined yards . . . and an NFL record (since broken) of 22 touchdowns.

During his first five seasons, Sayers was one of the most electrifying running backs in NFL history—so good that he was voted to the all-time team in the NFL's fiftieth anniversary season. But that is when his career all but ended after he suffered a devastating injury to his left knee in 1970.

However, that was not enough to keep him from being the youngest player ever elected to the Pro Football Hall of Fame. Those who see films of his runs today still marvel at his talent. Sayers was a marvel, a whirling dervish with the ball who left frustrated tacklers lying in his wake. His 6-foot, 200-pound frame belied great power.

Rosey Grier, the Rams' great defensive tackle of the 1960s, recalled an 80-yard touchdown run by Sayers: "I hit him so hard, I thought my shoulder must have busted him in two. I heard a roar from the crowd and figured he had fumbled. There he was, fifteen yards away, going on in for the score."

Gale Sayers

RUNNING BACK

Sterling Sharpe . . .

• Was an All-America at South Carolina, where he set records for catches and receiving yards.

• Was the Packers' number-one draft pick in 1988.

• Had 55 catches in '88, the most ever by a Packers rookie.

• Entered the 1994 season having caught at least one pass in 87 consecutive games.

• Became the first player to win back-to-back NFL receiving titles since the Chargers' Kellen Winslow in 1980-81.

• Surpassed Don Hutson as the Packers' number-two all-time receiver in 1993.

• Had 24 100-yard receiving games at the start of play in '94.

Sterling Sharpe doesn't just catch passes. He collects them in bundles.

Sharpe became the only receiver in NFL history to catch more than 100 passes in two consecutive seasons when he grabbed 112 for the Green Bay Packers in 1993, breaking his own NFL record of 108 set in 1992.

The 1993 season wasn't easy for Sharpe. He injured his toe so badly that he couldn't practice for the last eight weeks. Prior to the injury, he had three 10-catch games, including 147 yards and 4 touchdowns against the Tampa Bay Buccaneers. He also caught 10 for 114 yards and a score against the Chicago Bears.

The most electrifying reception of Sharpe's 1993 season didn't count toward the 112. With just 55 seconds to play in a first-round playoff game against the Detroit Lions, he caught a 40-yard, game-winning touchdown pass from Brett Favre. It was his club-playoff-record third scoring catch. The following week, in a playoff loss to Dallas, he gained another 128 yards on 6 catches.

Sharpe rapidly is striding his way up the record ladder at Green Bay, where great receivers such as Pro Football Hall-of-Fame inductee Don Hutson, Boyd Dowler, Max McGee, and James Lofton own most of the records. Sharpe has led the NFL in receptions three times, including 1989, his second NFL season, when he caught 90 for 1,423 yards.

Entering the 1994 season, he had caught 501 passes, second in Packers history (behind Lofton, with 530), for 7,015 yards and 47 touchdowns. He achieved the 500 mark faster than anyone in club annals.

O.J. Simpson . . .

• Carries the given name of Orenthal James Simpson.

• Had a then-record three 200-yard rushing games in 1973 en route to his 2,003-yard season.

• Passed the 2,000-yard mark on his thirty-fourth and last carry in the final game of the 1973 season, a 7-yard run off tackle against the New York Jets.

• Never failed to give credit to his offensive line, "The Electric Company" (so named because it "turned on The Juice").

• Finished his 11-season NFL career with 14,368 all-purpose yards, including 11,236 rushing.

• Set an NFL single-game record with 273 rushing yards in a 1976 Thanksgiving Day game at Detroit. It later was surpassed by Chicago's Walter Payton.

• Was constantly compared to Jim Brown, then the all-time NFL rushing leader. Simpson's opinion at that time: "In his day, Jim Brown was, without a doubt, the finest running back around. But I think today, I am the finest running back around."

He was O.J. . . . or "The Juice."

The last name really wasn't necessary. O.J. Simpson was one of those rare athletes who was known nationwide by his first name only.

The Juice was a two-time All-America and a Heisman Trophy winner at USC when the Buffalo Bills made him the first pick in 1969. He was a most unhappy rookie playing in a broken-down old stadium on the frozen tundra of Buffalo—and for a coach, John Rauch, who ignored his two NCAA rushing titles and declared at the outset, "I won't build my offense around one back, no matter how good he is."

Simpson was more than good. He had world-class speed; he was big enough at 6 feet 1 inch and 212 pounds; and he could flash three or four moves to get into the open before he had even passed the linebacker's position.

During his first three NFL seasons, Simpson averaged 642 rushing yards per season, and was more effective returning kickoffs than running off tackle. On the verge of retiring after a knee injury, he got a new life when Lou Saban, who ardently believed in the "big gun" theory—"if you have a big gun, you keep firing it"—became head coach in 1972.

For the next five years, mostly in new Rich Stadium, Simpson dominated NFL defenses, averaging 1,540 yards per season. In fact, he averaged 1,164 per season for the rest of his career, including two injury-plagued years with San Francisco. He became the first runner to gain 2,000 yards in a season when he rolled up 2,003 in 1973, notching one of his four NFL rushing titles.

Only injuries stopped the big gun from firing.

O.J. Simpson

RUNNING BACK

Mike Singletary . . .

• Averaged 15 tackles per game at Baylor, setting a school record with 232 as a junior.

• Was *Associated Press* NFL defensive player of the year in 1985.

• Had 2 fumble recoveries in the Bears' Super Bowl XX blowout of New England.

• Was a unanimous all-pro selection in 1986.

• Accumulated more than 1,400 tackles, more than 800 of them solo, during his NFL career.

• Played in 10 Pro Bowls and was named NFL Man of the Year in 1990.

• Was a first-team linebacker on the NFL Team of the '80s, as chosen by the Pro Football Hall of Fame board of selectors.

NFL fans never will forget Mike Singletary's eyes, which became a favorite close-up shot for TV directors. As the cameras zoomed in and captured Singletary's intensity, the eyes reflected the fire that drove this undersized middle linebacker during 13 NFL seasons.

Size, or the alleged lack of it, never was a detriment to Singletary's performances. He set a school record with 662 tackles at Baylor, and twice was named Southwest Conference player of the year—a rarity for a defensive player. Chicago thought so highly of the two-time All-America that it swapped second-round picks with the 49ers to get him in 1981.

Singletary earned a starting job in the seventh game of his rookie season and played in 73 consecutive games before injuries forced him to miss two during the 1986 season.

Though he played alongside high-profile defenders such as Richard Dent and Wilber Marshall, Singletary was the glue that held the Bears' defense together. He was their unabashed leader, particularly during the 1985 season when they won 15 of 16 regular-season games and eventually beat New England 46-10 in Super Bowl XX. "We can't survive without conflict, as crazy as that sounds," Singletary once said. "Without conflict, we are not the Bears."

Fortunately, Chicago had Singletary as a stabilizing influence.

You still can see him lined up before a play, leaning forward on his toes, eyes round as saucers but never blinking until the ball was snapped. He was coiled for action.

Bruce Smith . . .

• Was used as a blocking fullback in some short-yardage situations during his rookie season.

• Scored a safety in Super Bowl XXV when he tackled Giants quarterback Jeff Hostetler in the end zone.

• Had 3 sacks and a blocked field goal in the 1991 Pro Bowl.

• Was named AFC Defensive Rookie of the Year by the NFL Players Association in 1985, when he led the Bills with 6½ sacks.

• Won the 1984 Outland Trophy as college football's top lineman.

• Was named to the "Team of the '80s" by a special panel of Pro Football Hall-of-Fame voters.

Bruce Smith

Defensive end Bruce Smith has been a dominating defensive player since the day he joined the Buffalo Bills as the first player selected in the 1985 NFL draft.

Smith, 6 feet 4 inches and 280 pounds, is Buffalo's prime defensive weapon, sometimes moving from his defensive end position to line up as a tackle. But he always has been most effective at right defensive end, attacking right-handed passers from their blind side. Despite going against the NFL's best tackles, he has accumulated a club-record 106 sacks in his nine seasons, ranking among the NFL's top 10 in that department.

"He has an unbelievably explosive first step," said Pro Bowl tackle Bruce Armstrong of New England. "He's relentless, and once you get into him you must stay on him because he has such great closing speed. He can get to the quarterback even when you think the ball should be gone."

Smith ranked second in the NFL with 19 sacks in 1990, when he was a unanimous selection as NFL defensive player of the year. He sacked New York Jets quarterbacks 3 times in one game, and in a game against the Colts, he sacked quarterback Jeff George 4 times.

"Most people think that because he's so quick, he has only an outside pass rush. But he's so powerful that he can bulldoze over you," said former Oilers quarterback Warren Moon.

Smith is double- and triple-teamed, and while he has pointed to that fact in the past when seeking recognition, he would be insulted if the opposition didn't play him that way. "I demand attention," he said. "I feel that the only way I'll get better is if I have at least two people on me. It makes me rise to the occasion."

Emmitt Smith . . .

• Set 48 school records at the University of Florida, where he gained 3,928 yards in three seasons.

• Was the first player in 53 games to rush for 100 yards against the Philadelphia Eagles when he did so in 1992.

• Ranks third among Cowboys rushers—behind Tony Dorsett and Don Perkins—with 5,699 yards going into the 1994 season.

• Won NFL rushing titles in 1991 (1,583 yards), 1992 (1,713), and 1993 (1,486).

• Gained 688 yards during a crucial five-game winning streak in 1993, averaging 138 yards per game and 6 per carry.

• Sparks Dallas's offense. In the final game of the season against the New York Giants, with the NFC East title on the line, he gained 229 yards (168 rushing, 61 receiving). Sixty-nine of those yards came after he had separated his shoulder but refused to leave the game. His running led the Cowboys to the winning field goal.

After missing the Cowboys' first two games of 1993—both losses—in a contract dispute, Emmitt Smith proved without a doubt that a quarterback's best friend is a great running back. After Smith returned, Dallas lost only two games the rest of the season en route to its second consecutive Super Bowl title.

"Defenses have to respect him," said Cowboys quarterback Troy Aikman, who knows all too well how much Smith means to his offense. "When they do, it opens up things for [wide receivers] Michael Irvin, Alvin Harper, and [tight end] Jay Novacek. If teams try to take away those receivers, we can run the ball up and down the field with Emmitt. With him in the lineup, we have a lot of weapons for a defense to think about."

What defenses think most about is Smith's running. Despite missing those first two games, and playing just one play in another, he won his third successive NFL rushing title with 1,486 yards in 1993. Smith, 5 feet 9 inches, 209 pounds, and powerfully built in his lower body, nearly became the first player in NFL history to get 1,500 yards three seasons in a row. He missed by 14 yards.

In Super Bowl XXVIII, Dallas's offense was dragging until the second half, when Smith got the ball 20 times and gained 91 yards as the Cowboys defeated Buffalo for the second consecutive year. His game totals were 30 rushes for 132 yards and 2 touchdowns. And as if all that isn't enough, the Cowboys were 39-1 when Smith carried the ball more than 20 times from 1990-93, and 29-1 when he gained 100 yards.

Now that's an impact player.

Bart Starr . . .

• Helped Alabama to the Orange and Cotton Bowls during his first two collegiate seasons, but did little thereafter and wasn't drafted by Green Bay until the seventeenth round in 1956.

• Completed 57.9 percent of his passes (83 of 142 for 1,069 yards and 11 touchdowns) in six NFL title games, one of the best big-game records in NFL history.

• Had career passing statistics of 1,808 completions in 3,149 attempts for 24,718 yards and 152 touchdowns.

• Made two huge pass plays in the Super Bowl: a 37-yard touchdown pass to Max McGee for the Packers' first score against Kansas City in Super Bowl I; and a 62-yard scoring pass to Boyd Dowler that gave Green Bay a 13-0 lead in its 33-14 victory over Oakland in Super Bowl II.

• Had a won-lost record of 82-24-4 during the eight years in which the Packers won or competed for NFL titles.

• Was elected to Pro Football Hall of Fame in 1977.

Bart Starr

Bart Starr almost was the invisible man during the Green Bay Packers' great championship run under coach Vince Lombardi. That's an odd thing to say about a team's quarterback. Yet Starr really didn't get the credit he deserved for the Packers' five NFL championships.

Starr had been in and out of the lineup during his three seasons prior to Lombardi's arrival. But when Lombardi watched Starr's previous performances on film, he determined that the former Alabama standout would lead the team. "My quarterback must be intelligent and unselfish," Lombardi said. "Bart has those qualities."

Lombardi raised Starr's confidence level to a point where the quarterback flawlessly ran the offense, which consisted of variations of a few runs and a few basic passes. Starr became so adept and confident in the system that he called nearly 50 percent of the Packers' offense at the line of scrimmage.

He became the full-time starter midway through the 1959 season and won the last four games, helping Green Bay to its first winning season in 12 years. He got the Packers into the NFL Championship Game in 1960, then rattled off NFL titles in 1961–62 and 1965–67. He was selected most valuable player of Super Bowls I and II after the latter two title runs.

Starr was a mistake-free passer, once going 294 attempts without an interception, and he won the NFL passing crown three times. His biggest play was a 1-yard quarterback sneak for the winning touchdown against Dallas on the Packers' final offensive play in the 1967 NFL Championship Game.

It wasn't flashy…but it was the mark of a winner.

Roger Staubach . . .

• Was college football's player of the year in 1963 while leading Navy to the Cotton Bowl and a top-10 ranking.

• Earned NFL player of the year honors and was MVP of Super Bowl VI after getting a starting job midway through the 1971 season.

• Produced 22,700 passing yards and 153 touchdowns for the Cowboys.

• Was admired by his coach, Tom Landry. "When you talk about great quarterbacks," Landry said, "Roger has to stand alongside Otto Graham and Johnny Unitas because he was so consistent and one of the great two-minute clutch performers, like Bobby Layne in his prime."

• In a playoff game against the 49ers in 1972, with Dallas trailing 28-13, he relieved Craig Morton and produced 17 points in the last nine minutes for a 30-28 victory. "I felt the only chance we had was to get Roger in there," Landry said afterward.

• Was voted to the Pro Football Hall of Fame in 1985. He and O.J. Simpson were the first Heisman Trophy winners to be enshrined.

One man was largely responsible for the Dallas Cowboys' "America's Team" label in the 1970s.

Roger Staubach was the most exciting quarterback of the '70s, a master of the impossible and the improbable. His ability to bring the Cowboys from behind to victory—he did it 23 times in the fourth quarter, 14 times in the final two minutes—captivated the nation and made Dallas fun to watch.

"Roger never knew when the game was over," tight end Billy Joe DuPree once said. "At the end of the game, even if we were down by twenty points, he'd be standing there by himself trying to figure out a way we could win it."

Staubach was a tenth-round pick of the Cowboys in 1964, though he faced four years of Navy service after a brilliant career at the U.S. Naval Academy, where he won the Heisman Trophy in 1963.

He attended Cowboys training camps during his annual leaves from the Navy and was a 27-year-old rookie when he made the team in 1969. But Staubach didn't become a starter until midway through the 1971 season, when the Cowboys were 4-3 and on the brink of collapse. Instead, he led them to their first Super Bowl victory, and in the next seven seasons took them to five NFC Championship Games and three more Super Bowls, including a win over Denver in Super Bowl XII. He had an 85-30 record as a starter and won three NFL passing titles.

You might call him "America's Quarterback."

Joe Stydahar . . .

- **Was a great player at West Virginia, where he made the All-East, Little All-America, and All-America teams.**

- **Always had great affection for George Halas. "George was like a second father to me," he said. "I really didn't know anything about football until I played for him. Whatever success I had, I owe to him."**

- **Told Halas he was "just about washed up as a player" when he sought to rejoin the Bears after World War II. "Put down any figure you believe is right on the contract," Stydahar told him. Halas wrote in $8,000, twice as much as he had paid Stydahar before the war.**

- **Was head coach of the Los Angeles Rams from 1950–52, leading them to an NFL title in 1951. He also coached the Chicago Cardinals in 1953–54.**

- **Was enshrined into the Pro Football Hall of Fame in 1967.**

Joe Stydahar epitomized the Chicago Bears' "Monsters of the Midway" during the late 1930s and early 1940s.

Nicknamed "Jumbo Joe," Stydahar was a 6-foot 4-inch, 230-pound tackle, large for an NFL player of that time. He had been a great two-way player at the University of West Virginia, yet linemen were little known even then, so most were shocked when George Halas made him a first-round selection in the NFL's first player draft in 1936.

Great players were at a premium in a rudimentary draft process, and running backs were the hot-ticket items. But Halas was building the Bears into a championship team, and he knew the foundation had to begin with a great line. His decision to pick Stydahar was backed by a solid recommendation from former Bears and West Virginia player Bill Karr, who had seen many of Stydahar's games. It turned out to be a brilliant move.

Stydahar was not only physically powerful, but always one of the Bears' fastest players. He was an aggressive 60-minute player, and no one in the NFL was tougher—he didn't even wear a helmet full time until late in his career.

Stydahar played on three NFL championship teams and five Western Division title teams from 1936–1942, and in 1945–46. He was in the Navy during World War II, and unlike many college and NFL players, didn't play service ball. The last game he played was the Bears' victory over the New York Giants in the 1946 NFL Championship Game.

Lawrence Taylor . . .

• Had 4 sacks and a forced fumble in his first training-camp scrimmage.

• Had a career-high 133 tackles as a rookie in 1981.

• Became the first defensive player ever named *Associated Press* NFL most valuable player in 1986. He had 20½ sacks among his 105 tackles that season, not to mention a 34-yard interception return for a touchdown against the 49ers in a playoff game.

• Feasted on Eagles. His chief sack victims were Philadelphia's Randall Cunningham and Ron Jaworski, each of whom he sacked 12½ times.

• Was a unanimous selection to NFL's Team of the '80s, picked by a board of Pro Football Hall-of-Fame voters.

• Recovered a fumble to set up Matt Bahr's game-winning field goal against San Francisco in the 1990 playoffs, sending the Giants to Super Bowl XXV.

• Had a total of 27 tackles, including 13 sacks, in four games against Washington and Philadelphia in 1986.

W hen God was creating pass-rushing linebackers, he had Lawrence Taylor in mind," then-Giants head coach Bill Parcells once noted.

Taylor, one of the NFL's greatest players during the 1980s, was rabidly appreciated by Giants fans, whose tradition of admiring great defenses went back at least 40 years to the Yankee Stadium days of the mid-1950s, when they introduced the cry of "Deee-fense, Deee-fense." During the '80s and '90s, Giants Stadium rocked with thunderous cries of "LT! LT!"

Taylor was an impact player who always seemed to play in a rage. Opposing teams had to double-team him with bigger tackles and guards because he was capable of slashing past them and bowling over running backs in his ferocious pursuit of quarterbacks.

If he believed a team was running its offense away from him deliberately, he took it personally and was determined to wreak havoc. The Giants often moved him from his usual spot at right linebacker to the left side, making it harder for offenses to avoid him.

Taylor, a number-one pick from the University of North Carolina in 1981, retired after the 1993 season when age and injuries finally reduced him to a level for which many NFL linebackers would settle. He finished his career with 132½ sacks, second all-time (not counting the 9½ that he recorded in his rookie season, before the NFL made sacks an official statistic). "I enjoy sacking the quarterback," he once said. "A sack is like a touchdown for the defense."

That being the case, he was the Giants' leading scorer for longer than a decade.

Jim Thorpe . . .

• **Was a Sac and Fox Indian, with some French and Irish heritage thrown in. His tribal name was Wa-Tho-Huck, which means "Bright Path."**

• **Was an All-America football player at Carlisle, where he earned five varsity letters in five sports during his senior year.**

• **Won the pentathlon and decathlon at the 1912 Olympic Games in Sweden. He was later stripped of his gold medals and trophies because he had accepted $15 a week to play a summer of semipro baseball. It was nearly 70 years before they were returned, long after he had died.**

• **Played major league baseball with the New York Giants. He was a good fielder, but he couldn't hit a curve ball.**

• **Played in the NFL with the Canton Bulldogs (1920, 1926), Cleveland Indians (1921), Oorang Indians (1922–23), Toledo Maroons (1923), Rock Island Independents (1924), New York Giants (1925), and Chicago Cardinals (1928).**

• **Was a charter enshrinee of the Pro Football Hall of Fame in 1963.**

I n 1950, the nation's sportswriters voted Jim Thorpe the greatest athlete in the first half of the 20th Century.

Much of that tribute was because of his exploits on the football field, first at the Carlisle Indian School in Pennsylvania, and later in professional football. He played with seven different pro teams in the American Professional Football Association and its successor, the National Football League.

But Thorpe's greatest days were with the pre-NFL Canton Bulldogs, who later became a charter member of the league in 1920. He was 27 years old when he signed with them for $250 a game, and he led the Bulldogs to "world championships" in 1916–17 and 1919, before they entered the APFA. So great was his appeal that Thorpe was elected league president in 1920. He served just one year.

Thorpe, whom college coach Glenn (Pop) Warner always said could have been even greater had he not been so indifferent to his great skills, was a true triple-threat runner-passer-kicker. He ran 100 yards in 10-plus seconds, and his open-field running was dynamic. "I gave them a leg for a second, then took it away," he once said.

The power in his 6-foot 1-inch, 190-pound frame was awesome. Knute Rockne, the legendary Notre Dame coach, played with Massillon for a time, and after tackling Thorpe for a couple of losses, was pulverized by the Native American on the third try. "It was as if a locomotive had hit me, and been followed by a ten-ton truck rambling over the remains," Rockne said later.

Thorpe was more of a gate attraction than a productive player after the NFL was formed. By that time, he already had become a national treasure.

HALFBACK

Y.A. Tittle . . .

• Was signed by the Cleveland Browns of the AAFC in 1948, but was traded to Baltimore to help the Colts stay competitive.

• Came to the 49ers in 1951 after a reshuffled Colts team had been disbanded following only one NFL season.

• Led the AAFC's Baltimore Colts to a division playoff as a rookie in 1948, and did the same thing with the 49ers in 1957 before they blew a 27-7 lead against Detroit in a playoff game.

• Played in six Pro Bowls, four with San Francisco.

• Amassed 28,339 passing yards, best in NFL history when he retired after the 1964 season.

• Rolled up 10,439 passing yards and 96 touchdowns in four seasons with the Giants.

• Became an assistant coach with the 49ers after he retired. When he stepped onto the field at Yankee Stadium before a game against the Giants, 62,000 fans gave him a standing ovation.

• Was enshrined in the Pro Football Hall of Fame in 1971, along with Giants teammate Andy Robustelli.

Just before the end of their 1961 training camp, the Giants sent second-year defensive lineman Lou Cordileone to the 49ers for 34-year-old quarterback Y.A. Tittle.

Cordileone was incredulous. His reaction—"Who else did [the 49ers] get beside me?"—later became one of sport's most famous queries, and it proved to be one of the greatest trades in Giants history.

Tittle—his given name was Yelberton Abraham—produced record numbers of touchdown passes and helped the Giants to three Eastern Conference championships in the last four seasons of his 17-year pro career. He enthralled sellout crowds at Yankee Stadium not only with his great talent, but with his fiery exuberance. They shook that fabled ball park with equal vigor if he threw a touchdown pass or ripped off his helmet and slammed it to the ground in disgust.

Tittle had seemed to be washed up when he was traded by the 49ers, who had gone to a Shotgun offense. But armed with great receivers such as Del Shofner, Joe Walton, and Frank Gifford, and backed by a great defensive unit, he helped resurrect Giants football.

Tittle, who retired with the same battered pair of shoulder pads he had worn at Louisiana State, set an NFL record with 33 touchdown passes in 1962, helped by a record-tying 7 in one game. He then broke his own mark with 36 scoring passes in 1963.

Tittle's greatest frustrations were losing the three NFL title games he started from 1961 to 1963; he lost twice to Green Bay and once to the Bears, on brutally cold days that helped to negate his team's great passing offense.

His individual accomplishments, however, will never be negated.

Emlen Tunnell . . .

• **Was the first black player ever signed by the New York Giants.**

• **Returned 46 kickoffs for a 26.4-yard average and 1 touchdown.**

• **Scored 10 touchdowns—5 on punt returns, 4 on interceptions, and 1 on a kickoff return.**

• **Was surprisingly productive. In 1952, the Rams' (Deacon) Dan Towler led the NFL with 894 rushing yards. Tunnell amassed 924 on interception, punt, and kickoff returns.**

• **Was chosen as a safety on the NFL's 50th anniversary team in 1969.**

• **Was a member of the Giants' famed Umbrella defense. Tunnell played free safety and was a deadly ball hawk.**

• **Still ranks second on the all-time NFL interception list, 2 behind Minnesota's Paul Krause, and still is first in career interception yardage with 1,282.**

• **Was defensive backfield coach of the Giants in the 1960s and '70s; he developed a fine secondary known as "Emlen's Gremlins."**

mlen Tunnell was told he never would play football again after breaking his neck in practice during his freshman year at the University of Toledo. In 1967, he was enshrined in the Pro Football Hall of Fame.

Following his football accident, he served three years in the Coast Guard, and after his military service, he went to the University of Iowa and won a starting job on defense. When the coaches refused to move him to running back, which he preferred, he left to seek a job in the NFL.

Tunnell walked into the New York Giants' offices, talked to owner Tim Mara, and walked out with a signed contract, one of the soundest investments the Giants ever made. He became an "offensive" force of his own with his work as a safety, and returning punts and kickoffs. "We don't play him on offense because he's more valuable to us right where he is," Giants coach Steve Owen once said. "With Em on defense, we have the potential to get the ball on any play in the game."

Vince Lombardi, who had been an assistant coach with the Giants, traded for the safety when he became head coach of the Packers. Tunnell helped Green Bay win the 1961 NFL championship.

When he retired after the '61 season, he was the NFL's all-time leading interceptor with 79.

Not bad for someone who couldn't play.

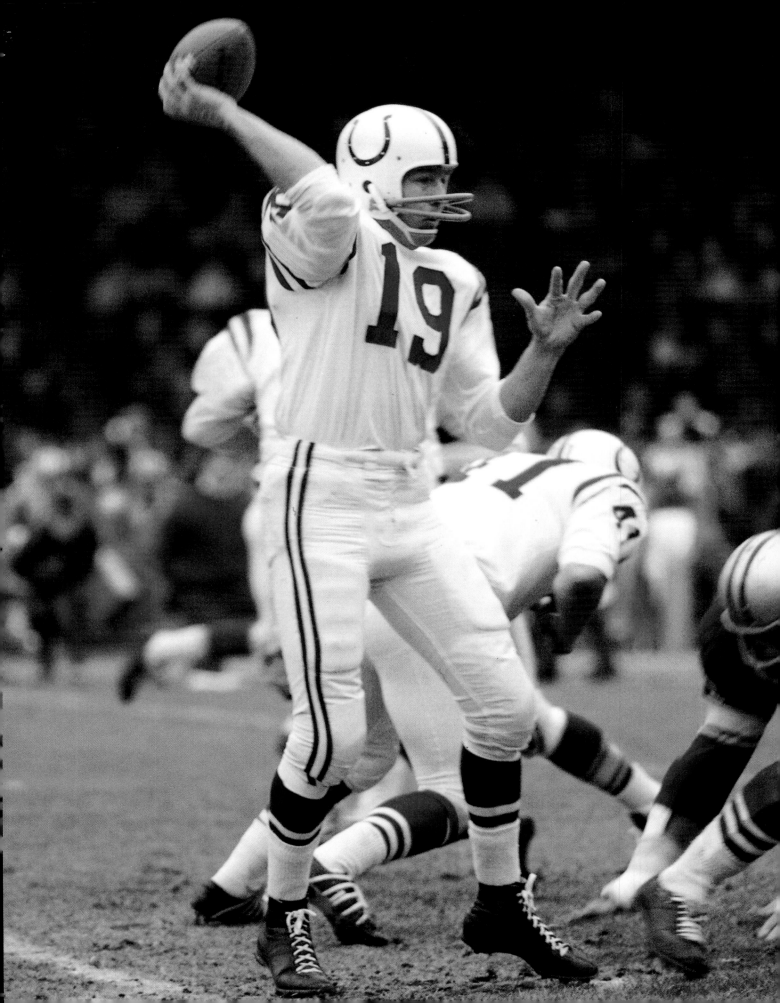

Johnny Unitas . . .

• Went to Louisville when Notre Dame and Indiana turned him down because of his size (6 feet 1 inch, 195 pounds).

• Backed up George Shaw in his first Colts season until Shaw was injured in the fourth game of 1956. Unitas did not relinquish the starting job until he was traded to San Diego in 1973.

• Had his first NFL pass intercepted and returned for a touchdown by the Chicago Bears.

• Accumulated 40,239 passing yards and 290 touchdown passes.

• Set an NFL record by throwing touchdown passes in 47 consecutive games.

• Won NFL titles in 1958–59 and was the starting quarterback when Baltimore won Super Bowl V.

• Was voted to the Pro Bowl 10 times and was most valuable player in three of the games. He also earned NFL player of the year honors three times.

• Was enshrined in the Pro Football Hall of Fame in 1979.

More than any player, Johnny Unitas is responsible for making pro football America's favorite sport.

During most of his 18 seasons of greatness in the late 1950s and throughout the 1960s, Unitas's daring play-calling and ability to win game after game in the final minutes—none more dramatic than the overtime 1958 NFL Championship Game against the New York Giants—coincided with television's marriage to pro football, and riveted America's attention to the sport for the first time.

Unitas, a ninth-round selection from Louisville in 1955, also was special because of his rags-to-riches story. Cut by Pittsburgh in 1955 without even throwing a preseason pass, he played semipro football for $6 a game with the Bloomfield Rams, near Pittsburgh. He got a second chance in Baltimore for $7,000 per season.

There was no denying Unitas's style. He was the ultimate competitor, tough as anyone who ever played. He wore crew-cut hair and hightop shoes, and he was the boss on the field. Mess up a play and he told you about it in the huddle. Give him time and he won the game.

Unitas worked hour after hour with great players such as Lenny Moore and Raymond Berry to perfect the Colts' precise passing offense. And he was always at his best when the game was on the line.

As Pro Football Hall-of-Fame defensive tackle Merlin Olsen once said of Unitas, "It isn't his arm or even his football sense. It's his courage."

Gene Upshaw . . .

• Faced his brother Marvin many times. Marvin was a defensive end who was a number-one pick of the Browns. Marvin later played with Kansas City and St. Louis.

• Played in three AFL and seven AFC Championship Games.

• Was offered $30,000 to sign as a pitcher with the Philadelphia Phillies when he left high school. He also had offers from Pittsburgh and Houston.

• Played in 207 consecutive games.

• Was the only Raiders player to play in the club's first three Super Bowls.

• Was all-AFL twice, all-pro three times, and played in seven Pro Bowls or AFL All-Star Games.

• Was enshrined in the Pro Football Hall of Fame in 1987.

• Became executive director of the National Football League Players Association after his playing days were over.

Gene Upshaw

A l Davis was concerned after the 1966 season. Davis, then the Raiders' general manager and part owner, had watched Buck Buchanan, Kansas City's 6-foot 7-inch, 280-pound defensive tackle, manhandle the left side of the Oakland Raiders' offensive line, and because his team would face Buchanan twice a year, Davis decided he needed some help. Fast.

Gene Upshaw, a first-round selection from Texas A&I in 1967, was the answer. At 6 feet 5 inches and 255 pounds, Upshaw became a prototype in the NFL's trend toward big guards. Most pro guards at the time were 6-1 or 6-2, 240 pounds, but fast and quick footed.

Upshaw was that, too. He ran a 4.7-second 40-yard dash and when he pulled out to lead the Raiders' favorite play—a sweep around left end—he was something to behold.

When he joined the Raiders, Upshaw was a relative football neophyte who hadn't played until his senior year in high school. But what he lacked in experience, he more than made up for physically and mentally. With his size and speed came a dogged work ethic and dedication to excel, abetted by his intelligence and ability to grasp the nuances of his position even before his rookie year had ended.

Upshaw played in Super Bowl II after his rookie season, against Green Bay's Pro Bowl defensive tackle, Henry Jordan. During the game, which the Packers won 33-14, Upshaw kept asking Jordan, "What am I doing wrong?"

Jordan remembered it well. "That kid was in there asking me what he did wrong," he said, "and all he did was kick the hell out of me. I kept asking myself, 'What if he does something right?'"

Norm Van Brocklin . . .

• Wrote to Rams owner Dan Reeves during his junior year at Oregon and told him he was ready to graduate early if the Rams wanted to draft him. The Rams drafted him in the fourth round in 1949.

• Still holds the NFL single-game passing record of 554 yards, set against the New York Yanks in 1951.

• Led the NFL in passing three times, and also led the league in punting twice, with averages of 44.6 and 43.1 yards in 1955 and 1956, respectively.

• Was renowned for having a great football mind. "What Van Brocklin did with that 1960 Eagles team was remarkable," Sam Huff once said. "They were strictly an average club with no running game, their offensive line was lousy, their defense was mediocre. Van Brocklin took them to the title."

• Completed 1,553 passes for 23,611 yards and 173 touchdowns in 12 seasons.

• Was voted to the Pro Bowl nine times.

• Was enshrined in the Pro Football Hall of Fame in 1971.

N orm Van Brocklin," Philadelphia tight end and former teammate Pete Retzlaff once said, "is three people, all of them perfectionists."

"The Dutchman," as Van Brocklin was nicknamed, was one of the unique stars in NFL history. He played quarterback with the Rams for nine seasons, helping them win their only NFL championship in Los Angeles with a fourth quarter, 73-yard touchdown pass to Tom Fears against the Cleveland Browns in 1951.

Yet he mightily resented the press corps for whipping up a quarterback controversy, first with Bob Waterfield (whom he replaced in the '51 title game), and later with Bill Wade. In 1955, Van Brocklin took the Rams to another championship game but lost to the Browns.

Fed up with the annual quarterback battle, he announced his retirement in 1957, but he came back the next season when he was sent to the woeful Philadelphia Eagles in that franchise's biggest trade ever. In 1960, he led the Eagles to the NFL championship, beating the Green Bay Packers 17-13 in the only playoff game coach Vince Lombardi ever lost.

There was no denying either Van Brocklin's talent or the fierce competitiveness that made him so great. Sam Huff, Pro Football Hall-of-Fame middle linebacker with the Giants, once said, "He was right in the middle of everything. He'd spit in your eye, call you every name in the book, then run your butt off the field. We used to hit him some wicked shots and he'd say, 'Is this as hard as you can hit, Sweetie?'

"I loved him."

QUARTERBACK

Steve Van Buren . . .

• **Was born in Honduras, where his father was a fruit inspector. Steve was orphaned as a child and lived in New Orleans with his grandparents.**

• **Didn't make the football team as a high school sophomore. He left school to work in an iron foundry for two years, then returned and won a football scholarship to Louisiana State.**

• **Didn't make All-America as a senior, so few NFL teams were interested in him. LSU coach Bernie Moore tipped off the Eagles, who surprised everyone by picking Van Buren on the first round.**

• **Gained 5,860 yards during his NFL career, which was cut short by a knee injury suffered during training camp in 1950.**

• **Averaged 11.2 yards on 45 receptions; 13.9 yards on 34 punt returns; and 26.7 yards on 76 kickoff returns. He scored 77 touchdowns.**

• **Also played defensive back and had 9 interceptions.**

• **Was enshrined in the Pro Football Hall of Fame in 1965.**

Steve Van Buren lined up as a halfback with the Philadelphia Eagles for eight seasons, but anyone who tackled him will swear he was a fullback. In the end, the position didn't matter. Van Buren was the NFL's best runner in the last half of the 1940s, when he won four rushing titles and brought the Eagles NFL championships in 1948 and 1949.

Van Buren was pure runner, whether from scrimmage or returning kickoffs and punts. He ran a 10-second 100-yard dash, and he was the first NFL player to record two 1,000-yard seasons.

His moderate size (6 feet 1 inch, 202 pounds) belied powerful legs that ripped apart tacklers' arms. During the summer, he strengthened those legs by tying 25-pound weights to his ankles and running mile after mile, up and down the soft dunes of the New Jersey shore.

Van Buren's most impressive season may have been 1945, when he won the "triple crown"—ranking first in rushing, scoring, and kickoff returns. But his greatness is underscored by what he did for his team. Before Van Buren arrived as a number-one draft pick from LSU in 1944, the Eagles never had finished higher than fourth place. He took them into the NFL Championship Game in 1947, where they lost to the Chicago Cardinals; and then to back-to-back championships over the Cardinals and Los Angeles Rams.

Van Buren was the difference in winning both titles. He scored the only touchdown as the Eagles beat the Cardinals 7-0 in ankle-deep snow, and when they defeated the Rams 14-0 in ankle-deep mud at the Los Angeles Coliseum, Van Buren carried 31 times for a record 196 yards.

HALFBACK

Randy White . . .

• **Was recruited by only three colleges, but he wound up winning the Outland Trophy and Vince Lombardi Award at Maryland in 1974.**

• **Set weightlifting records with the Cowboys, bench pressing 470 pounds and cleaning and jerking 375. White, who added 50 pounds to become a defensive lineman, ran a 4.7-second 40-yard dash.**

• **Had an unofficial 16 sacks in 1978, an incredible number for an interior lineman who was double- and triple-teamed on every play.**

• **Was a pain for former Eagles guard Pete Perot, who waged some classic battles with him: "He had great quickness to go with his tremendous upper-body strength. He had so many ways to beat you that it got very frustrating at times."**

• **Was named to the Pro Bowl nine times. Also played in three Super Bowls.**

• **Was drafted by the Philadelphia Phillies as a pitcher in high school, but his father encouraged him to play college football instead of baseball.**

Cowboys safety Charlie Waters had it right when he once described defensive tackle Randy White. "He's a manster," Waters said, "half man and half monster."

White successfully reprised the role of Pro Football Hall-of-Fame member Bob Lilly when he was moved to right defensive tackle after three seasons of drifting around the Cowboys' defense at linebacker and defensive end. In White's first season as a starting tackle, he and Harvey Martin were selected as co-most valuable players of Super Bowl XII.

White, a first-round draft pick in 1975, figured to be a Dick Butkus-type middle linebacker following an All-America stint as a defensive end at Maryland. He also was tried at outside linebacker, but his lack of backpedal skills on pass defense finally convinced Dallas coach Tom Landry that White was best suited to be a lineman.

White immediately built himself up to 275 pounds, and no one ever played the position better. He often was compared with Lilly because of his great speed and strength. He was double- and triple-teamed constantly, and he returned the "compliment" by scattering blockers who either couldn't handle his strength or were beaten by his great quickness.

"Many times he blew past me so fast I didn't even know he was there," said John Dutton, who played next to White for several years in the Cowboys' "Doomsday II" defense.

White thrived on defensive line combat. "When Randy lined up on you, he didn't care whether you were all pro or a rookie," Landry said. "You got the same treatment—and that's what made him unique."

Randy White

DEFENSIVE TACKLE

Reggie White . . .

• Was an All-America at Tennessee in 1983, earning the nickname "Minister of Defense."

• Had 23½ sacks in two USFL seasons.

• Led the way for Philadelphia in a 1992 first-round playoff game, stopping 265-pound Saints fullback Craig Heyward near the goal line to force a field goal, and later sacking Bobby Hebert for a key safety in the Eagles' victory.

• Had an NFL-best 21 sacks in 12 nonstrike games during the 1987 season.

• Has been named Defensive Lineman of Year by both the NFL Players Association and the NFL Alumni Association.

• Had 11 sacks in 1989 to help Philadelphia set a club record with 62.

• Was the object of a massive "treasure hunt" as a free agent after the 1992 season. He finally signed with the Green Bay Packers for more than $17 million. "He is maybe the finest player who has ever played his position," Packers coach Mike Holmgren said when White was signed.

At 6 feet 5 inches, 285 pounds, and with a deep, gravelly voice, Reggie White often seems larger than life to the casual observer. Imagine what he must seem like to a harried quarterback.

White has given plenty of them fits during his 11 seasons in pro football, nine in the NFL after two seasons with the Memphis Showboats of the United States Football League.

Going into the 1994 season, White was the NFL's all-time sack leader with 137—the same number of games he has played with the Philadelphia Eagles and Green Bay Packers. He was with Philadelphia from 1985 to 1992 after being a number-one pick in a supplemental draft of USFL players.

White is an amazing athlete. He played a 20-game season with Memphis in 1985, then moved into the NFL a few weeks later and played 13 more games with the Eagles.

His impact was immediate. In his first game, against the New York Giants, he had 2½ sacks and a pass deflection that led to a touchdown by Herman Edwards. At season's end, White shared the team lead with 13 sacks and was a unanimous all-rookie selection. He led the NFL with 18 sacks in 1988 and was the keystone of the Eagles' defense when it led the NFL in fewest rushing, passing, and total yards allowed in 1991. Constantly double-teamed, he often lines up as an interior lineman to help free others for an outside pass rush.

White has played in eight Pro Bowls, including seven with Philadelphia. He was MVP of his first Pro Bowl—following the 1986 season—after getting a record-tying 4 sacks.

DEFENSIVE END

Larry Wilson . . .

• Was a seventh-round selection from the University of Utah, where he played running back and defensive back.

• First was tried at running back by the Cardinals, but asked to be switched to defense after his first practice session. He then worked at cornerback, but found himself on the bubble after giving up 3 touchdown passes to Colts end Raymond Berry in a preseason game.

• Is the Cardinals' all-time interception leader with 52.

• Led the NFL with 10 interceptions in 1966, including a seven-game streak with at least one. He got the Bears' Rudy Bukich 3 times in one game during that streak.

• Played in eight Pro Bowls and was named all-pro six times.

• Scored 8 touchdowns (including 1 as a running back) and a safety during his career.

• Was enshrined in the Pro Football Hall of Fame in 1978, his first year of eligibility.

One of the most precise plays in football is the safety blitz. Larry Wilson, the man who did it first, also did it best—along with most other elements of defensive secondary play.

Wilson thought he was on the brink of being cut in the final preseason game of his rookie 1960 season. But he played in place of regular free safety Jimmy Hill, shut out the 49ers' best wide receiver, R.C. Owens, and started in the season opener. Wilson didn't relinquish the job for 13 years.

Wilson and the safety blitz always have been synonymous. It was the brainchild of Cardinals defensive coach Chuck Drulis, who needed only the right person to execute it. The maneuver demands precise timing because the safety must start running 15 yards from the line of scrimmage—without tipping off the quarterback—and arrive the moment the ball is snapped. "I enjoyed it," Wilson once said. "It was a chance to get back at the quarterback. He stands around all day smiling at you."

It also took its toll. Wilson played with broken bones, chipped teeth—even with two hands in splints from a 1965 game against the Giants in which he had his left hand smashed between the helmets of two offensive linemen, then broke a finger on his right hand. The following week, wearing the splints, he leaped high to intercept a pass against Pittsburgh, saving a victory for his team.

Pat Summerall, who played against him with the Giants and later broadcast many of his games, said it best: "You can run out of superlatives talking about Larry Wilson. To me, he typified everything great you could possibly expect from a football player."

Kellen Winslow . . .

- Was an All-America in 1978 at Missouri, where he caught 71 passes for 1,089 yards and 10 touchdowns in four years.

- Wound up with the Chargers by the scant margin of 10 seconds. San Diego swapped first-round spots with the Cleveland Browns in the 1979 draft just 10 seconds before the turn expired.

- Ate up the Raiders with 100 career catches for 1,153 yards, including a career-high, NFL-record-tying 5 touchdown receptions during a 13-catch day in 1981.

- Led the NFL with 89 receptions (for 1,290 yards) in 1980 and 88 (for 1,075) in 1981.

- Had a career-high 15 catches against the Packers in 1984. His best yardage game was 171 on 10 catches against Pittsburgh in 1980.

- Caught at least 3 passes in all but one game during the 1983 season.

- Was all-pro in 1980-81-82, and was voted to five Pro Bowls.

- Was elected to the Pro Football Hall of Fame in 1994.

The millions of fans who watched tight end Kellen Winslow's heroic performance for the San Diego Chargers in a 1981 AFC playoff game against the Miami Dolphins learned forever the true meaning of "pro football warrior."

Winslow was helped to the sidelines, totally exhausted, several times on that hot, wet, muggy afternoon in the Orange Bowl. Revived with a quick breather and some oxygen, he went back out and continued the battle. At game's end, he left the field under the support of two teammates after performing as well as anyone in playoff history—he caught 13 passes for 166 yards and blocked a potential winning field goal on the final play of regulation, forcing overtime. San Diego eventually won 41-38.

Winslow was the right tight end in the right system—the Chargers of coach Don Coryell and quarterback Dan Fouts, a group that made opposing defenses squirm under new, liberalized passing rules. Winslow caught 541 passes for 6,741 yards, and he caught them in bunches (26 games of 100 or more yards).

He was a perfect fit in this pass-happy system, where the tight end's chief responsibility was catching the ball, not blocking. He was sure-handed; he had sprinter's speed; and at 6 feet 5 inches, he towered over defensive backs. He also played with great wide receivers such as Charlie Joiner and John Jefferson, which opened up myriad opportunities in opposing secondaries.

There was no tight end like him before, and there hasn't been one since.

Photo Credits

Page 8: John Biever; **page 9**: NFL Photos; **page 10**: John McDonough; **page 11**: James D. Smith; **page 12**: NFL Photos; **page 13**: NFL Photos; **page 14**: Wide World Photos; **page 15**: NFL Photos; **page 16**: Vernon Biever; **page 17**: NFL Photos; **page 18**: Walter Iooss; **page 19**: NFL Photos; **page 20**: Malcolm Emmons; **page 21**: Malcolm Emmons; **page 22**: NFL Photos; **page 23**: The Stiller Co.; **page 24**: Tony Tomsic; **page 25**: Malcolm Emmons; **page 26**: Tony Tomsic; **page 27**: Tony Tomsic; **page 28**: Richard Raphael; **page 29**: Carl Skalak; **page 30**: Peter Read Miller; **page 31**: George Gojkovich; **page 32**: NFL Photos; **page 33**: NFL Photos; **page 34**: J. Soohoo; **page 35**: George Rose; **page 36**: NFL Photos; **page 37**: Darryl Norenberg; **page 38**: Peter Read Miller; **page 39**: Scott Cunningham; **page 40**: Paul Spinelli; **page 41**: Paul Jasienski; **page 42**: Dan Rubin; **page 43**: NFL Photos; **page 44**: NFL Photos; **page 45**: NFL Photos; **page 46**: NFL Photos; **page 47**: NFL Photos; **page 48**: John Biever; **page 49**: R. H. Stagg; **page 50**: NFL Photos; **page 51**: NFL Photos; **page 52**: NFL Photos; **page 53**: Darryl Norenberg; **page 54**: Richard Raphael; **page 55**: Tony Tomsic; **page 56**: Malcolm Emmons; **page 57**: George Gojkovich; **page 58**: NFL Photos; **page 59**: NFL Photos; **page 60**: Peter Read Miller; **page 61**: Peter Read Miller; **page 62**: Vernon Biever; **page 63**: NFL Photos; **page 64**: Pro Football Hall of Fame; **page 65**: NFL Photos; **page 66**: NFL Photos; **page 67**: NFL Photos; **page 68**: Tony Tomsic; **page 69**: Tony Tomsic; **page 70**: M. V. Rubio; **page 71**: Tony Tomsic; **page 72**: Vic Stein; **page 73**: Detroit Lions; **page 74**: Rob Brown; **page 75**: Photostaff; **page 76**: Frank Rippon; **page 77**: George Gellatly; **page 78**: James F. Flores; **page 79**: NFL Photos; **page 80**: George Rose; **page 81**: Aggie Skirball; **page 82**: Malcolm Emmons; **page 83**: Michael Zagaris; **page 84**: Vic Stein; **page 85**: Nate Fine; **page 86**: Darryl Norenberg; **page 87**: NFL Photos; **page 88**: Peter Read Miller; **page 89**: Al Kooistra; **page 90**: Frank Rippon; **page 91**: NFL Photos; **page 92**: George Rose; **page 93**: Michael Zagaris; **page 94**: NFL Photos; **page 95**: NFL Photos; **page 96**: Pete J. Groh; **page 97**: Paul Jasienski; **page 98**: NFL Photos; **page 99**: NFL Photos; **page 100**: NFL Photos; **page 101**: NFL Photos; **page 102**: Vernon Biever; **page 103**: Tony Tomsic; **page 104**: Malcolm Emmons; **page 105**: Tony Tomsic; **page 106**: James F. Flores; **page 107**: R. H. Stagg; **page 108**: Malcolm Emmons; **page 109**: R. H. Stagg; **page 110**: NFL Photos; **page 111**: John Biever; **page 112**: Peter Brouillet; **page 113**: Gerald Gallegos; **page 114**: Greg Trott; **page 115**: Bill Amatucci; **page 116**: Scott Cunningham; **page 117**: Bob Rosato; **page 118**: Herb Weitman; **page 119**: Malcolm Emmons; **page 120**: Bob Rosato; **page 121**: Bob Rosato; **page 122**: Carl Skalak; **page 123**: George Gojkovich; **page 124**: Malcolm Emmons; **page 125**: Paul Spinelli; **page 126**: James D. Smith; **page 127**: Gerald Gallegos; **page 128**: Chris Schwenk; **page 129**: Allen Kee; **page 130**: Malcolm Emmons; **page 131**: Tony Tomsic; **page 132**: Tony Tomsic; **page 133**: James F. Flores; **page 134**: NFL Photos; **page 135**: NFL Photos; **page 136**: Louis Raynor; **page 137**: Bob Rosato; **page 138**: NFL Photos; **page 139**: Pro Football Hall of Fame; **page 140**: Russ Reed; **page 141**: Tony Tomsic; **page 142**: NFL Photos; **page 143**: New York Giants; **page 144**: J. Makita; **page 145**: Malcolm Emmons; **page 146**: Mitchell B. Reibel; **page 147**: Tony Tomsic; **page 148**: Sports Illustrated; **page 149**: Pro Football Hall of Fame; **page 150**: NFL Photos; **page 151**: Philadelphia Eagles; **page 152**: Tony Tomsic; **page 153**: Al Messerschmidt; **page 154**: Michael Yada; **page 155**: Vernon Biever; **page 156**: Herb Weitman; **page 157**: Rob Brown.